© Oluwakemi O. Ola-Ojo
2015

TO THE GROOM WITH LOVE
ISBN: 978-1-908-015-10-5

1st Printing 2015

© 2015 by Oluwakemi O.Ola-Ojo
All publishing rights belong exclusively to Protokos
Publishers.

Published by,
Protokos Publishers
London
United Kingdom
Web E-Mail: admin@protokospublishers.com

Layout design: Resorel Designs (info@redsorel.co.uk)

*Printed in the United Kingdom. All rights reserved under International Copyright Law. Contents and/or cover may not be reproduced in whole or in part in any form without the express written consent of the Publisher.*

*To the Groom with Love*

## CONTENTS

- Dedication — vi
- Acknowledgment — vii
- Preface — viii
- Introduction — xi
- The Disobedient Lover — 15
- The Praying Lover — 32
- The Take Over & Humble Lover — 42
- The Exposing Lover — 54
- The God Fearing Lover — 67
- The Unwary Lover — 73
- The Redeeming Lover — 86
- Poems: — 92
- Have You Gotten to the Well? — 92
- Where do you pick your choice? — 94
- Alone with God. — 96

*To the Groom with Love*

# DEDICATION

To grooms all over the world.
To my brothers and brother-in-law.
To all married men of every race, age and colour.

*'Love is very fragile; handle it
with care and prayer'*

## ACKNOWLEDGEMENT

I have been privileged to listen to great men and women of God teach and preach the word of God from my conception to date. They are too many to list but I would like to thank them all for sowing God's words into my life.

My greatest thanks is to my parents - Rev. Dr William and Mrs. Grace Ojo who though did not have much material wealth when we were growing up but daily taught my siblings and myself the word of God. They live what they preached and taught. In God's words that we were brought up to believe and live, today I have been able to write this book under the anointing of the Holy Spirit.

My thanks also to the editors for good editing. I thank the team at Protokos Publishers for the hours spent on this project and for marketing my books.

Finally and most important to my readers who make our writing projects worthwhile. May the Lord meet each one of us at our points of needs in Jesus name. Amen.

## PREFACE

In 2007, The Lord helped me to write and release the book titled "To the Bride with Love' which has been well received worldwide and has been a blessing to many individuals, families and communities. Almost immediately came the request for a similar book for the 'groom'.

I had to wait to hear from the Holy Spirit not only to give the confirmation but also to name the men that are featured in this book. Just as its counterpart has been a blessing to all who found time to read it; so I pray that this will bring immeasurable blessings to each man, groom, husband and father in Jesus name. Amen.

*To the Groom with Love*

## Proverbs 31: 10-31

*New International Version (NIV)*

*10 [b] A wife of noble character who can find?*
*She is worth far more than rubies.*
*11 Her husband has full confidence in her*
*and lacks nothing of value.*
*12 She brings him good, not harm,*
*all the days of her life.*
*13 She selects wool and flax*
*and works with eager hands.*
*14 She is like the merchant ships,*
*bringing her food from afar.*
*15 She gets up while it is still night;*
*she provides food for her family*
*and portions for her female servants.*
*16 She considers a field and buys it;*
*out of her earnings she plants a vineyard.*
*17 She sets about her work vigorously;*
*her arms are strong for her tasks.*
*18 She sees that her trading is profitable,*
*and her lamp does not go out at night.*
*19 In her hand she holds the distaff*
*and grasps the spindle with her fingers.*

*To the Groom with Love*

*20 She opens her arms to the poor*
*and extends her hands to the needy.*
*21 When it snows, she has no fear for her household;*
*for all of them are clothed in scarlet.*
*22 She makes coverings for her bed;*
*she is clothed in fine linen and purple.*
*23 Her husband is respected at the city gate,*
*where he takes his seat among the elders of the land.*
*24 She makes linen garments and sells them,*
*and supplies the merchants with sashes.*
*25 She is clothed with strength and dignity;*
*she can laugh at the days to come.*
*26 She speaks with wisdom,*
*and faithful instruction is on her tongue.*
*27 She watches over the affairs of her household*
*and does not eat the bread of idleness.*
*28 Her children arise and call her blessed;*
*her husband also, and he praises her:*
*29 "Many women do noble things,*
*but you surpass them all."*
*30 Charm is deceptive, and beauty is fleeting;*
*but a woman who fears the Lord is to be praised.*
*31 Honor her for all that her hands have done,*
*and let her works bring her praise at the city gate.*

*To the Groom with Love*

## INTRODUCTION

*The Bible says: 'Can two walk together unless they agree?' For most people, finding the right person to marry could be very challenging and unnerving. The reason for this is not far-fetched. Under normal circumstances, most people get married once in their lifetime. Therefore it is not a great surprise that most people find searching for a suitable spouse very intimidating.*

As human beings we are constantly making and taking decisions. We make some as individuals whilst others are made on our behalf. Of all the major or significant decisions a person can make, choosing a spouse to marry in my opinion is next to that of giving one's life to Jesus Christ. It is a major decision that is often made in adulthood, one made consciously, one that is not to be taken lightly, one that soon afterwards the decision maker can begin to enjoy or regret.

Some people are made in their marriage, others are destroyed. No wonder the Bible says 'He who finds a wife finds what is good and receives favor from the Lord' (Proverbs 18:22). How does a person find the right person when the Bible says 'the heart is deceitful above all things, and desperately wicked: who can know it?' (Jeremiah 17:9, KJB).

## To the Groom with Love

There is a popular saying that beside (or behind) a successful man there is a successful woman. Many by the grace of God have had positive influence over their wives and vice versa and others have been ruined or killed by their spouses. Together in this book, we will look at the lives of seven men in the Bible who got married under different circumstances similar to those that men experience nowadays. They married from different backgrounds and to different women and their families. With the help of the Holy Spirit we shall examine how these men found their wives, the effect of their choices on their lives, careers and their families, and we shall also examine the roles of the husband in the marriage.

Why seven? That was the number of men that the Holy Spirit gave me and He chose for me the men to write on. Seven stands for perfection, for example, seven days in a week.

### *God ordained marriage*

God has ordained the man to be the head of his home. Marriage for anyone and everyone is a new beginning. No longer would individuals in the relationship be expected to see themselves and reason as singles but as a joint entity that will very regularly refer to themselves in the plural form 'we'. Each person in the relationship now has to accommodate, love and consider the other person. Imagine you the man trying to find the right spouse for yourself. Where do you begin your search? What should you be looking for in your choice? How do you know when you have met the right woman? What if she turns you down? What are your roles in the marriage as the husband?

You need to marry a woman who has a purpose and destiny in life

## To the Groom with Love

-a woman who is hardworking, forward looking, forward planning and industrious. The woman must be one who prepares for all times and seasons, the future even the night times. The person must be a woman who understands her calling whether it is at home, in the office or in the market. On your part as the groom and husband, you need to be sure of yourself and come across, as a person that is not intimidated by his wife's success for example, as her success ultimately will be her spouse's success. You must be a man who will allow his spouse to become all she has been created to be.

To the Groom with Love is written for the young man (or not so young) who is searching for the right woman to marry. It is written for a man who is about to get married or a man who has just been married to a woman with the hope of the groom learning from some grooms in the Bible. This book will be handy to all married men.

Imagine you having a once in a lifetime opportunity of meeting seven men who were once faced with the challenge of finding their own wives and raising their own families. Over the next seven days each person will be taking you out for an evening walk. And whilst you are taking the walk perhaps on a cool beach, or around your favorite spot, each of them will tell you his story and experience but will begin with a verse or two of scriptures that are relevant to the situation you are currently going through. At the end of each walk, each of the men will pray with you.

They will visit you in the order of their appearance in the Bible.

*The Disobedient Lover*

*Fear God, and keep His commandments;
for that is the whole duty of everyone.
Ecclesiastes 12:13b.*

*To the Groom with Love*

# The Disobedient Lover

You are rightly dressed and ready for an evening walk and talk but you are wondering who will be coming. Just then there is a knock on the door. On opening it, your guest who is well advanced in age asks if you are ready to go. You quickly answer, "Yes" and close the front door to walk with this old man and here is what he says:

Young man, 'Commit your ways unto the Lord and lean not unto you own understanding, in all your ways, acknowledge Him and He will direct your path' (Proverbs 3:5-6).

> *Firstly, to begin, we need to have a relationship with the Lord our Maker. Only the Maker of a thing has predetermined the strength, purpose and end of the thing. God has our dossiers in His Hands. He alone knows the way we should go and what we should do be doing at each time and place. Take time to pray seeking the face of the Lord and avail yourself of good and godly counsel. There is a Sunday song written by Sidney Cox that says '*
> > *My Lord knows the way through the wilderness*
> > *All I have to do is follow.*
> > *My Lord knows the way through the wilderness*

*The Disobedient Lover*

*All I have to do is follow.*
*Strength for today, is mine all the way*
*And all that I need for tomorrow.*
*My Lord knows the way through the wilderness*
*All I have to do is follow.*

http://www.path2prayer.com/article/992/revival-and-holy-spirit/books-sermons/new-resources/my-lord-knows-the-way

Secondly, we need to commit our ways unto the Lord in every matter of life. At various points in life everyone needs to be carried. God is the only one that is able to carry us securely and safely through life. He is concerned about all that has happened or will happen to us. Our understanding of things and people are often shallow and could be influenced such that the real thing or person is unknown because of the mask they put on. God knows the end before the beginning. Lean not on your own understanding, in all your ways acknowledge Him. God knows all that is to be known about anything and anyone. His ways and thoughts are very different to the way we perceive things as human beings. As we moment by moment acknowledge Him, He is able to direct our ways towards the right path. My brother, your own God-ordained wife maybe near or far away but until the Lord opens your eyes to see her, you might be looking in the wrong direction or dating the wrong person.

Thirdly, when God directs our paths, we are spared so much heartaches, failures, wasted time and efforts. With our God, success is inevitable even in marriage. To find a woman of noble character, you should also be a man of exalted moral excellence.

Fourthly, God created man to have dominion over all of His other creatures. He gave man the task of looking after the garden and naming all of His creatures. As you prayerfully seek Him and fulfill His purpose for your being, God will direct your path in finding the right woman to marry.

### *Now to my story…*

In the beginning God created the heaven and the earth in five days and on the sixth day God made man in His own image primarily that man might have dominion over all of His creation to rule on earth as He God is ruling in heaven. The purpose of creating man also is to have fellowship with God and that man might worship Him (Genesis 1:26-28). God then put me, Adam, in the beautiful garden He had made, to look after it and equally, to give names to all of the animals that He created. Whatever name I called the animal or bird has ever since been their names. Our God is a God of order and orderliness. As you go into finding a suitable wife and getting married, learn to be organised. Find God's purpose for your life first and set your heart to it with all diligence.

### *Your pronouncements are weighty*

Be careful what you call situations and events that come into your relationship and marriage. For out of our mouth comes death or life as you carry God's DNA and genes. God spoke all into being and they all remained as He had pronounced them. It might be easier or more comforting to say the negative but it is more rewarding to speak life and God's words only into your marriage and family. For any negative situation or condition that might arise in your marriage, you need to remember to use the name above all names to tackle it. Always remember that God blessed mankind at creation and so you are not cursed.

You need to depend on God for a wife and suitable helpmeet for you. God knows that it is not good for any matured man to be alone; He designed marriage and companionship in the first instance. As you take time to do the things of God, He will in His mercies lead you to the right woman.

In God providing me with a wife, God made me to sleep first and removed one of my ribs, from which Eve was made. Brother, our God exposed Eve to me and I immediately recognised her and accepted her as mine. She was the only woman then and I could have rejected her but I knew immediately as soon as I saw her that she was mine. Today there are millions of ladies of marriageable age, some of whom you might come across in the course of your daily tasks, directly or indirectly, and if you will depend on God He will direct you in making the right choice in Jesus name.

### *God gives a suitable helper*
God gave me a suitable helpmate created from my rib bone and

close to my heart to love and cherish, not from any bone from my head so she could rule over me or my legs so that I could step on her. You need a helpmate suitable to meet your needs, not a dictator, a destroyer, killer, liability or a destiny contender. God gave me an 'Eve to marry not a Steve'. Be sure that you both have medical check-ups before your marriage and confirm that your wife to be is indeed biologically a female. Take time to know yourselves and try to identify what sort of woman will be suitable to you in your calling and purpose in life. Marry a helpmate not a destroyer of purpose, talent, mission, destiny and anointing. Choose to marry a friend not an enemy. Remember marriage as ordained in the Bible is for life as long as both of you live. Marriage for us as Christians is a covenant and commitment not a contract.

To identify your wife, you will need to know and understand yourself and prayerfully consider what qualities you are looking for in your helpmate. Score these qualities according to your priorities. Whilst you alone know the physical qualities of the woman, perhaps this write up might help you find the spiritual quality you want in your future wife.

## AND WHO IS YOUR IDEAL WOMAN?

*A man who finds a good wife finds favour from the Lord*
*In the midst of many women within and outside the Church*
*How do you go about choosing a wife my brother?*
*Charm is deceptive and beauty is fleeting,*
*But a woman who fears and honors the Lord*
*Is to be praised and rewarded.*

*Many men's lives have been enhanced or destroyed*
*Simply by their choice of marriage partner*
*Whilst some are being blessed, others are being cursed.*

*The task of choosing a wife, beloved, is compounded today*
*Within our society of fast life and instant relationships*
*Internet datelines and ungodly exposures.*

*Choosing a wife my brother, needn't cause you fear*
*If you will humbly set time aside to seek God's face*
*In prayers and reading the scriptures for whom your ideal woman is.*

*Is your ideal woman beautiful, thoughtful, wise, and generous like Abigail?*
*Who though married to a foolish man, with wisdom interceded for her family?*

*Is your ideal woman like Deborah, the mother, wife, prophetess, and judge?*

## To the Groom with Love

*Who in bravery went to war to encourage the army general against the enemies?*

*Is your ideal woman like Delilah?*
*Who throws a tantrum to find the source of your strength?*
*Yet conniving with your enemies to destroy the man she claims she loves?*

*Is your ideal woman like Elizabeth who remained dedicated to the Lord?*
*In spite of her barrenness was faithful to God and had a child in her old age?*

*Is your ideal woman like Eve, the helpmate for Adam?*
*Who by conversing with the devil ate the God-forbidden fruit?*

*Is your ideal woman like Gomer, Hosea's wife, the professional prostitute?*
*Who was unfaithful and kept seeking after other men though married.*
*She had to be bought back very often by her husband from her lovers?*

*Is your ideal woman like Hagar, the slave and victim of circumstances?*
*Though she gave an heir to Abraham, got sent away due to pride,*
*But sought the Lord and heard Him in her very trying times?*

*Is your ideal woman simple like Hilda?*
*Who was a prophetess that heard from God concerning her country?*

*Is your ideal woman like the orphaned, beautiful and obedient Esther?*
*Who in wisdom took counsel on what to wear thus becoming the chosen queen.*
*She prayerfully put her life on the line so that her race might be saved.*
*She approached the king in her royal outfit, fed him and exposed her enemy.*

## The Disobedient Lover

*Is your ideal woman like Leah who though lacked physical beauty was fruitful*
*And also lived to support their husband after her sister's death?*

*Is your ideal wife like Lydia the prominent seller of purple clothes and believer?*
*Though away from home on a business trip went to fellowship on Sabbath*
*Got baptized with her family and entertained the apostles in her home?*

*Is your ideal woman like Mary or Martha, Jesus' friends, and Lazarus' sisters?*
*Who loved their brother so much and sent for Jesus when Lazarus was ill*
*Who listened to Jesus and entertained Him often in their own home?*

*Is your ideal woman like caring Miriam who watched over baby brother Moses?*
*Got him the best nurse available, later became the prophetess and singer?*

*Is your ideal woman like Priscilla, the hospitable and welcoming tent Maker?*
*Who regularly opened her home to Paul, his companions, and other believers?*

*Is your ideal woman like the beautiful but striving Rachel the shepherdess*
*Who for the love for her husband stole her father's idols?*

*Is your ideal woman like Rebecca, the woman who was hospitable to Abraham's servant?*
*Who comforted Isaac when his mother died, and prayed to God when pregnant?*

*Is your ideal woman like the kind Ruth who would accept your God as her God?*
*Supporting your family with all her God-given abilities as long as she lives?*

*To the Groom with Love*

*Is your ideal woman like Sarah, the blessed mother of all nations?*
*Whose barrenness God turned into laughter even in her old age?*

*Is your ideal woman like young, engaged Virgin Mary who loved God so much?*
*She was willing to let the Lord's will be done at the cost of losing her fiancé?*

*Charm can be deceptive; beauty can be vain dear brother*
*But a woman who fears the Lord is to be adored and praised.*
*As you place your desire for your ideal woman before the Lord*
*Trust Him to lead you to this woman in His own way and time.*
*For a man who finds a good wife finds favor from the Lord.*

Once you have prayerfully identified your future wife, get godly counsel and be married according to your faith and culture if that is not contradictory to the word of God.

To establish a godly and peaceful home, you will need to explain to your wife and your household any God given instructions and directions. God's instructions as contained in the Bible and revealed personally to us periodically or daily are for our good and benefit. God is not a joy-killer but a joy-giver. He knows the end before the beginning. He loves us enough to forewarn

\* *Proverbs 31:30, Genesis 2:18-25.*

us of the danger spots ahead if we care to listen and obey Him. Prayerfully, get your wife and family to understand your God given instructions, and directions and what roles each must play individually and how you all can obey God's instructions.

All was very well with Eve and I as a couple until Eve began to have conversations with the devil. My unwary wife was persuaded by the devil that came in the form of a snake to eat of the forbidden tree. The snake twisted God's instructions for us about the fruit until she agreed with the snake and ate out of what was forbidden. We all need friends but there is a wise saying that reads 'Show me your friends and I will tell you about your destiny or future'. You need to prayerfully and wisely take time to find out who the person is that your wife has been hanging around with, what messages or suggestions are being drummed into her hearing. If they are things that will make you and your family go to hell or disobey God, then pray and seek godly counseling without any delay. Beware of your own or wife's friends who claim to want to help her and you but who is set to make you both disobey God and thereby lose your relationship with God and each other. Run away from such friends and evil associates.

One day, without my permission, the snake invariably lured my wife to pluck from the forbidden tree and eat one of its fruits. She then gave me some of the fruit to eat and I did eat. Whilst my wife was deceived, I wasn't. Our eyes became opened; we saw ourselves as naked and embarked on covering up. We became much afraid especially of God when He next visited. Before then it was a visit we both eagerly awaited but once we disobeyed we became very much afraid of God and His presence. Be focused, a woman may be easily deceived but you as the man shouldn't. Choose to obey God and His instructions in its entirety than succumb to your wife's 'forbidden fruit feed'

Avoid touching or tasting whatever God has forbidden – it will only lead to death. Sin usually appears appealing, harmless, promising, pleasurable, eye-catching and fulfilling but in the end destroys. Please avoid sin at all cost, as the price for sin is too much. Our sin automatically removed God's covering from us and that made us feel vulnerable therefore our embarking on trying to cover ourselves up.

I disobeyed God. Disobedience is the greatest and most costly sin such that God promised our redemption there and then. God had set our boundaries in the garden but I chose to listen to my wife by eating the forbidden fruit rather than obeying God. Brother, love God and obey Him at all times and in all situations. Nothing should stand between you and your Maker. God held me accountable and He will hold you accountable for everything that happens to your family.

When confronted by God or people or the result of your sins or mistakes, rather than making any attempts to rationalise the blunder or blame someone else or something else, you need to acknowledge the sins, and confess them. You ought to be humble to ask for forgiveness from God or anyone that has been wronged. Looking back now, if I had asked for God's forgiveness rather than shifting the blame to my wife, perhaps God's punishment would have been less severe.

Avoid what I call 'the blame game' in your marriage as it leads to nowhere. When asked by God why I had eaten the forbidden fruit I said '…the woman you gave me' Eve also blamed the serpent. Eve and I lost our rights to remain in the Garden of Eden, I had to toil before we could eat, and Eve was going to have pains at childbirth. God is good and kind but He is also just. You might confess your sins but may have to face the consequences of your sins.

Please let me share with you the following true statements:
- All disobedience gets paid for.
- Destruction follows disobedience in most cases.
- Disobedience often leads to isolation from loved ones and places.
- Disobedience will always take one back to where one does not want to be.
- Often the parent pays for the disobedience of the child and the child pays for the disobedience of the parent.
- The disobedient person and their loved ones and associates are vulnerable to attacks following the act of disobedience.

- The cure for disobedience is the shedding of the blood of a replacement. Jesus paid the ultimate price for all sins including disobedience; so go to Him and confess your sins.

It does not matter the income of your wife or her wealth, you as the husband should be the breadwinner providing for the needs of your family. The Bible says a man who does not provide for his family is worse than an infidel (1 Timothy 5:8).

### *Pray for your offspring*
Bring up your child to love God and know how best to worship God with their talents, time and treasures. Teach your children the importance of giving God a worthy offering. Pray against sibling rivalry too. Eve and I were blessed with Cain and Abel. When both grew up, they presented their sacrifice as offerings before the Lord. Cain's offering was rejected whilst Abel's offering was accepted. God warned Cain of his anger and jealousy but Cain did not take God's counsel but went ahead to kill his brother. What we had thought was a harmless disobedience repeated itself in the family with the loss of an obedient dear son and the banishment of the other! The pain of losing a child and the banishment of the other is something that no parent should have to experience.

### *God will restore*
Finally I can tell you that our God is faithful to all of His promises. Whatever you lose in your marriage, God is able to

replenish. With Cain now banished and Abel dead, I could not but wonder which seed of ours could now bruise the serpent's head (Genesis 3: 1-19; especially verse 15). Surprisingly when we least expected, God gave Eve and I another son named Seth; and with him came a new beginning (Genesis 4:25– 26). God is able to give you and your wife a new beginning whenever you need one if you will both turn to Him.

We have now walked back to my home and I invite Papa Adam in for a drink. After we had shared the drink together, he gave me my favorite fruit in the box and prayed with me saying:

> *Dear Father and our Maker, It is with a heart of gratitude that we come to You tonight; first for the gift of life, for creating us and for being our Father. I am grateful for the opportunity of sharing some of my experiences with Your son_____ (insert your name). Help him first to discover his purpose in life and pursue it according to Your will. Thank You Father for keeping him to this age when he needs to have a wife. Father I pray that You in Your mercies will grant Your son_____ (insert your name) Your favour and please lead him to the right helpmate for him in Jesus name.*

*Please Father keep him and his wife from everyone or everything that will lead them into disobeying You. Help him and his wife to first be each other's best friend and have God fearing and God loving friends, please grant him the wisdom and ability to provide for the needs of his family. Help him and his wife to raise godly children. Whatever they lose in this marriage, because of Your mercies, please replenish. In Jesus name we have prayed with thanksgiving. Amen.*

### *Reflections*

I saw Papa Adam to the door thanking him for his visit and with my favourite fruit in my hand I begin to recount all that he said to me - that:

- I should find God's purpose for my life first.
- I should depend on God for a wife. God knows it is not good for a man to be alone.
- I should prayerfully identify my own God-given wife - a helpmate not a purpose, talent, mission and anointing destroyer.
- I should explain to my wife and household our God-given instructions and support them to obey God always.
- I must beware of friends who may claim to want to help my wife and I but who are set to make us both disobey God, thereby losing our relationship with God and each other.
- I should be focused. A woman may be easily deceived but I, as the man must not.
- I should choose to obey God and His instructions in its entirety than succumb to my wife's ungodly alternative.

- I must avoid touching or tasting what God has forbidden as it only leads to death.
- I must avoid playing 'the blame game' in my marriage.
- I should bring up our children to love God and know how best to worship Him with their talents, time and treasures.
- I must pray that any present and seemingly harmless sin will not wait for our seed to destroy in future.
- I should pray against sibling rivalry and untimely death.
- I am meant to be the breadwinner and my wife being a helpmate.
- When and where I, my wife, children or anyone in my household have sinned, Lord please help me to take the full responsibility, and in humility ask for Your forgiveness. I should lead others in my household to repent of their sins before the Lord.
- I should realize that I would be held accountable for all that happens in my family, good or bad.

*The Praying Lover*

*Seven days without prayer,
makes one weak*

*To the Groom with Love*

# The Praying Lover

You are still thinking about your unique walk with Papa Adam yesterday and ready for the walk and talk today when you hear a very gentle knock on the door. Who can it be today?

Opening the door you are greeted by a soft-spoken, handsome, immaculately clean and wealthily dressed man. He returns your greeting and proceeds to say:

> *With thanksgiving let your request be made to God*
> *(Philippians 4:6).*
> *One will chase a thousand and two will chase ten*
> *thousand. Deuteronomy 32: 30*

### *Significant Decisions Require Specific Prayers*
In life we make daily decisions varying in degree of significance, some more highly signicant than others. Some decisions we make ourselves, and others are made on our behalf. One of such significant decisions is who to marry. Whether you make this decision or it is made on your behalf, you as the groom need to spend quality time in the place of prayer. With thanksgiving, let your request be made to God. In prayers you can describe to God what sort of helpmate you desire. Take this from me: God will surprise you positively about your request.

Whilst you end your prayers with God's will be done, please be more specific about things that are important to you and your destiny. It might be a mismatch for a politician to marry a very quiet and introverted person or for a marine engineer to marry a lady who is unable to solve simple domestic challenges such as changing light bulbs by herself.

There is a saying in Africa that good things demands prayers and bad things also need prayers. Prayers to the only wise and Almighty God will be more successful if you and your wife pray together. For the Bible says in that one will chase a thousand and two will chase ten thousand. Also Mathew 7:7-8 says whatever two of us will agree together on earth when we pray about it will be done by our Father in heaven. My brother, please marry from within the household of faith, and as early as possible spend quality time with your wife in prayers. Marry a woman who fears the Lord, as this will protect her, you, and the family in all things.

### *Now to my story…*
My name is Isaac, the only son of Father Abraham and Mother Sarah. My parents were friends of God. God called dad and mum out of the land of Ur to relocate to Canaan. God also promised them a son and eternal generational blessing. However I was not born until twenty-five years after the initial promise and covenant; when all hopes had been lost, and when mum and dad were very old. Mum was 90 years old at the time of my birth and dad was 100 years old.

*To the Groom with Love*

I was the only son of multimillionaire dad and mum, the covenant son and the covenant of blessing carrier, inheriting all of my parent's wealth, servants and assets, and the heir to all my parents' assets. I was 40 years old when my father called his most trusted servant and gave him the responsibility of finding a wife for me. I was not allowed to go on the journey to our homeland to seek for her myself because God had said when He called my father that he was not to return to Ur again; so dad also forbade me to go on this trip.

What if she was not the right woman for me? As you can imagine, there were many what 'ifs' in my mind. All I could do was to take time to pray for godly direction that this man would find me the right woman. I could not reject whoever he brought and I prayerfully went along with my father's wishes for the type of wife. I approached God in prayers and meditation for I knew only God could give me a sensible wife as a gift (Proverbs 19:14). Thank God the servant's trip was successful and he found me the right woman - humble, highly hospitable and very beautiful like mum. I learned to know and love her intimately after she arrived.

In certain cultures or families it is still customary for them to have arranged marriages, especially for the son, the heir to the throne or family fortune. The family clearly sets out the criteria of whom their son could marry. If you are blessed to come from such a culture or family, may I say that it is not barbaric; for many times if not all, your family would have conducted their own research and choose the best woman for you. Equally you should realise that they are finding you the right wife in love, and they are trying to protect your interest from all unpleasant surprises or marital failures. All you could is to make your request about the type of wife you want unto God who is still able to lead aright.

Would you like to have a designer, custom-made and fit for purpose wife; a suitable, loving, caring, humble and obedient wife? Then call unto God earnestly and honestly. Call God and tell Him your request in faith with thanksgiving. What He did for me, He is able and willing to do the same for you.

Finding a wife for you in such an instance is many times out of love and goodwill so that the family values, treasures and perhaps faith can be managed and maintained. A woman who does not share or respect your family values may end up devaluing the same and ultimately destroy it. A woman who does not share your faith cannot join you in loving, trusting and serving your God. She may even lead you astray in trying times.

What are some of your good family values that you will like to extend into you upcoming family? In Papa Abraham's household, walking with God whatever it took, being hospitable, teaching the children and household in faith, rescuing families in trouble, paying tithes, giving sacrificially were some of the values. List the godly values in your family, which you would want to see continuing in your marriage.

Twenty years into our marriage, Rebecca and I though married as virgins, were still barren! Blessings are often generational, and may be dependent on our walk with God. Brother, please note that generational blessings or curses often run in families. As soon as I realized this, I went unto the Lord to intercede for my wife, and guess what? God blessed us with a set of twin boys, Esau and Jacob. Our God is forever faithful and good (Genesis 25:20-21). Don't be surprised that some problems that are traceable generationally from your family or wife's family may try to raise their ugly head in your marriage. Don't give in or give up; just find time to seek the face of the Lord and intercede. Whatever makes you or your wife uncomfortable, disturbed, disheartened, sad or sleepless is a sure sign of your need for intercession.

I allowed Rebecca to comfort me when my mother died. In the journey of your marriage, there will be ups and down, happy and challenging moments, mind boggling and energy sapping events. In all of these, please give your wife the opportunity to prayerfully minister to your needs, pains and weaknesses.

Though in theory I was a multimillionaire before my birth, yet I enjoyed working alongside of dad, learning and gleaning from his wealth of wisdom and after dad's home call, I re-dug the wells, giving them the names that dad had earlier given them. Surely, *there is life and wealth in the well (Genesis 26:15-22). Brother, whilst it is desirable to be born into a wealthy family, it is more rewarding to also work for your own wealth and have good administrative and managerial skills to manage the family fortunes. An untrained child will sell off the family inheritance if care is not taken. An African proverb puts it this way: 'Omo ti a o ko loma gbe ile ti a ko ta,' meaning 'An untrained child will sell the family's landed property,

Walking and working with God will put you in an enviable position amongst others. I encountered a lot of jealous opposition digging the wells but at last God overcame our enemies and we started to prosper (Genesis 26:24) Brother as you prayerfully conduct your affairs and business, you will surely win over all your enemies in Jesus name, opposition notwithstanding. Be a peace seeker in every hostile environment you might find yourself.

Many often wondered how I could sow in the time of famine and in the same year reap a hundred fold returns. Simple. These are some of my secrets:

- Totally rely on God and trust Him for directions on what to do.
- Do not allow famine to determine if and where you relocate to.
- Be careful on what you give to God and how.
- Pay your tithes and give offerings with a cheerful and obedient heart.
- Be at the forefront of technology in your career or business and use the tested or upcoming technology to your advantage.

Unlike our colleagues in the farming business, we used irrigation on our crops rather than wait for rain, and sowing at the right

---

*There is more on the exposition of 'There is life and wealth in the well in 'Good Dads, Bad Dads' by Oluwakemi Ola-Ojo. ISBN 978-1-908-015-94-5. Check it out @ www.amazon.co.uk/com

time. With God's blessing, we were successful.

In my old age when my eyesight was not as good as when I was younger, I was tricked by Rebecca and Jacob to give Esau's blessings to Jacob but nevertheless I blessed Esau (Genesis 27:1-40). No one knows the time of death. Brother, please make it a daily habit to bless your family. There is anointing and life in your tongue. I blessed Jacob the next heir in line and sent him to the right place to look for a wife.

Finally avoid two things in your marriage: First, showing favoritism; for it is a killer to family and sibling unity. Second, avoid comparing your wife with your mum or any female relative. It would only bring jealousy and unnecessary competition and tension.

### *Pa Isaac Prays*
We arrived back at home just in time for a well-deserved drink with Pa Isaac. My mind was just bubbling over such an amazing talk. After our drinks, Pa Isaac gave me a praying mat and he prayed for me saying:

Oh God, the Father of Papa Abraham, myself, my son Jacob and our eternal Father, it is with joy that I present to You, Your son _____(please insert your name) this evening who is about to embark of the journey of marriage. Thank You Lord for You ordained the ministry of marriage. Thank You for finding him a helpmate and helpmeet. Father may the light of his prayers and intercession not be quenched but enhanced and multiplied in this marriage. May You be the third person in this relationship. May You hear him when he intercedes on behalf of his wife and family. May You cloth him with honour and dignity, wisdom and peace. May You enlarge his coasts and surround him with Your divine protection. My Father please bless all the good works of his hands and grant him a godly heir to carry on Your generational blessing upon his family. May he never be barren in the fruit of his loins or the fruit of his wife's womb, or barren in ideas, nor barren in the works of his hands in Jesus name we have prayed with thanksgiving. Amen.

### *Reflections*
You gratefully see Pa Isaac to the door thanking him and as you lay down to sleep, your mind begins to recollect what Pa Isaac said to you:

- It is not barbaric to have arranged marriages; it is common in certain cultures or families. Where this is often done it is a sign of love and protection of the heir to the throne or family inheritance. Rather than force, he suggests that such a man prayerfully went along with his father's wishes of type of wife.
- I may only get to know fully and love my wife post wedding.
- Generational blessings or curses often run in families. Blessings can be enhanced with prayers and curses can be averted, stopped or changed by prayers.
- Whatever causes my wife or our children or me any distress calls for my prayer of intercession. Prayers can overcome every problem. Nothing works as fast as prayers.

- I must be a prayerful husband and father, engaging my wife in prayers of agreement according to the will of God.
- I should allow my wife the opportunity to prayerfully minister to my needs, pains and weaknesses. My success is my wife's success so we should celebrate together too.
- Whatever wealth I inherit is no reason for me not to work or not to be hard working. I need to learn all that I need to know about my job or inheritance and how best to manage it.
- I need to create and use technology to my advantage.
- I should be a peace-seeker in every hostile environment.
- There is life and wealth in the well. I may have to re-dig them.
- I should learn to bless my wife, children and household daily.
- With my blessings I should point our children especially the next heir-in-line in the right direction of how and where he can find the right spouse for him.
- I must avoid favoritism - the killer to family and sibling unity.
- I must avoid comparing my wife with my mum or any female relative, as it brings jealousy and unnecessary competition and tension.

Soon you drifted into a good and well-earned sleep.

The Take Over & Humble Lover

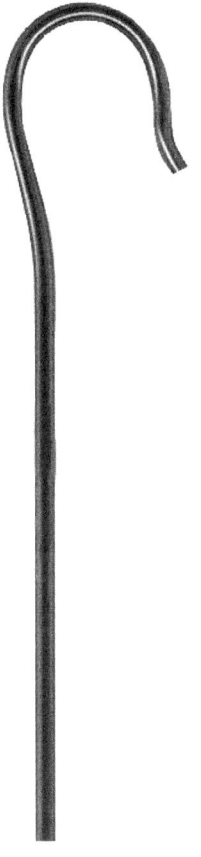

*God's rod's and staff will comfort me.*
*Psalm 23:4 NIV*

*To the Groom with Love*

# The Take Over & Humble Lover.

*'Show me a great man of God and I will show you a very humble man'*

*Humility is the acid test for the greatest.*

Your walk and talk with Papa Isaac yesterday was such an eye-opener and you are looking forward to your guest today. Just as you are wearing your shoes there is a gentle knock on your door. As you turn the knob on the door open an elderly man with a long white beard, holding a rod in his hand, greets you.

You shut the door behind you and join him in what has become your routine evening walk. "Who is this patriarchal figure?" you are wondering. As if he could read your mind, he calls you by your name and says I am Moses and he begins to talk to you:

For this reason a man will leave his father and mother and be united to his wife, and they will become one flesh (Genesis 2:24, Matthew 19:5, Mark 10:7-8. NIV 1984).

*The Take Over & Humble Lover*

Marriage is for matured men not for boys. A man who is not ready to leave his parents and be united to his wife in my opinion is not ready for marriage. Marriage is a significant rite; a new beginning for both groom and bride For the groom, one that requires him to be united with his wife. You will have to learn to protect, provide for and love your wife unconditionally. Once you say 'I do' to the marriage vows, it ends your running to mum and dad like a boy. Learn to take along from your parents all the good and helpful behavior and value systems. Learn from them but leave behind your parent's failures and weaknesses.

Be prepared as your wife will look for love and godly directions from you. It is your responsibility to provide for her and your new family. There is power in unity. Make every effort to be in unity with your spouse.

**Now to my story…**
I was born by Hebrew parents but raised as an Egyptian prince. The circumstances surrounding my birth and stories from my biological parents made me realise that I was meant to deliver my people from the Egyptian oppression and slavery. In the few years that I was with my biological parents, I was taught and I learnt the Hebrew culture and language. As an unmarried Egyptian prince at the age of forty years wanting to set a Hebrew slave free, I mistakenly killed an Egyptian whom I felt was being wicked to an Israelite and covered his corpse in the sand. But somehow Pharaoh heard and sought to kill me because of the murder. Brother………, no matter how deep you conceal your

sin, it will be exposed with time and the right environment so run to Jesus Christ, repent of the sin and confess it today to Him.

I fled into exile in the wilderness. Running for days, I finally made it to the outskirts of one Midian town where I helped some shepherdesses water their flock at the well and defended them against other shepherds. They thanked me and went their way. Their father, Reuel, a priest of Midian, enquired how they got home earlier than their usual and they told him about me – the Egyptian prince they had met. Their father asked that I be invited to their home and I was offered a place to stay. Whilst there, I learnt their language and way of life. I availed myself the opportunity of mentorship from my father-in-law.

### Be helpful and humble
Brother, please be helpful to as many as you can in life. With time I got married to one of the ladies and took over the care of the sheep from then. I found my wife Zipporah, Reuel's daughter, in the land of my sojourn. Learn to be humble in life and be helpful to your wife and in-laws. Should you for whatever reasons have to live with your in-laws and your wife or in-laws are temporarily supporting you, try not to abuse their generosity but be a blessing in every way possible. Learn to be the husband and father of the home once you are married. Certain responsibilities that your wife carried before might now be yours. Be glad to take over such and give it your best shot.

### Spend time with your children
Brother, please spend meaningful and purposeful time with

your children. First, teach them their origin- from God and from heaven. Teach them to have a meaningful relationship with their Maker. Teach them the nature and culture of God and let them know God wants us to be like Him in every way and at every time. Teach them the culture of heaven, love of God and obedience to God and His dictates, godly love rightly expressed unconditionally one to another, respect and preservation of life not otherwise etc.

Take time to teach your children about their roots especially the good things about their rich culture. Teach them to eat your food, wear your traditional clothes (weather permitting). Help them to understand, speak, be able to read and write in your language. God did not make a mistake about your origin, and no culture is more superior to the other. Appreciate and celebrate it so long as it does not contradict the word of the Lord. The 'Moses' in your child needs to know and identify with their spiritual and biological roots otherwise God's calling may never be realised in their life. A race or people that deliberately and totally disrespect, deny, devalue and destroy their tradition and good culture will soon be extinct.

Teach the word of God from as soon as possible in the life of your child. Children can and are able to understand the message of the gospel if we but teach them. They don't lack intelligence; they simply need teachers. Roots are important. Teach honoring God every time, everywhere and in every situation. The time we have as parents is limited as the child will soon be off to school, college or university. And before you know it they are gone!

They become adults in their own rights with responsibilities for a new generation they have got to groom and prepare for life.

### *Be curious*

For forty years I served my father in-law, tending his sheep and I took regularly the sheep to the mountains. I was once a prince and heir to the throne of Egypt, but now I have become an unpaid shepherd. It was not unusual to occasionally find the bush burning due to the hot temperature and the heat from the mountain. The fire would die down after consuming the bush. On a normal day whilst tending my father in-law's sheep, I noticed a particular fire but the bush was not burning. I decided to turn aside to look and find out why this was happening. My brother, inquisitiveness sometimes leads to discovery. God will always use an event, a thing, or a people to call your attention to Himself. Turning aside to see what was happening, I heard my name being called. I instantaneously knew it was God calling me. Every creature instinctively answers to his or her creator.

Then came the instruction from God that I should remove my shoes for I was standing on a holy ground. God's presence made the ground to be holy but it was hot and the ground certainly was very hot. In humility and reverence, I took off my shoes. Standing barefooted in His presence yet my feet were not burned. Indeed in His presence there is fullness of joy and at His right hand are pleasures forever more. Psalms 16:11b. My brother, just as I had to take off my physical shoes before God's presence and before He would give me His instructions and directions, so must you today take off your spiritual shoes of every sin you have committed. You must take off your shoes of comfort and trust God for His divine instructions, revelations and directions.

### *The great assignment*
In spite of all my excuses to God, there and then God commissioned me for a great assignment, which was for me to return to Egypt to set His people free. All the years of self-examination, unpaid service to my father in-law, caring for my father in-law's helpless sheep was to prepare me for my life's assignment. Brother………, until one find's one's mission or purpose in life, life may be meaningless and void. My sin of murder and other mistakes notwithstanding, God was still willing to use me. My stammering was equally not a problem with God, who qualifies those He chooses to call. My own human approach of setting my people free forty years ago was no match for God's divine plan (Romans 8:28, Numbers 23:19).

God spoke to me in the Hebrew language from then onwards even though I was fluent in at least three major languages – the Egyptian, Hebrew and Midian languages. God chose to speak to me in the language of those He was sending me to. The shepherd's rod in my hand became God's rod from then on. Whatever tool you have in your hand when touched by God becomes your own 'God's rod'. Your pen, your cheque book, your asset, your car, etc. Once touched by God, whatever you have becomes your own God's rod to be used to destroy all the works of Satan in your life, family and community.

Once I had received God's revelation, I took time to discuss God's commission and assignment for me with my wife and in-laws; and they gave their approval for my return to Egypt. Brother, if you have been living with your in-laws or friend or colleague or another relative, when it is time for you and your family to leave them, please do so with their understanding and blessing. Don't burn the bridge of the relationship for you might need it later.

It was good that my wife understood my Hebrew culture and the calling of God upon my life, for on our way back to Egypt when the angel tried to kill me, my wife quickly remembered to circumcise our sons and my life was spared. Take the time to share with your wife and family about your background and your faith.

Brother, please realise that life is a journey that is often in stages or phases (Ecclesiastes 3: 1 – 8). My first 40 years I spent as an Egyptian prince, the next 40, I spent in the backside of the Wilderness University as a shepherd. I spent my last 40 years fulfilling God's destiny for my life and that of leading the people of Israel out of Egypt to the Promised Land. Whatever stage of life you may be in, please stay focused and be close to God. May you never start your life assignment ahead of God's timing and place in Jesus' name. God's purpose for your life may be delayed but it shall surely be fulfilled in Jesus name. (Amen)

Please keep a healthy relationship with your in-laws. My father in-law was very helpful to us after we left Egypt especially in navigating our way through the wilderness and he was particularly full of wisdom when he came to see us in the camp. The old man gave me a very useful advice for attending to the needs and demands of the people. My father in-law taught me the importance of job sharing and empowering others so that I could use my time more profitably for God and His people. Your in-laws may not have had any formal education or training, and might even be very poor, but they could possess a wealth of useful experiences that you can learn from if you are humble enough to listen and carry them along.

### *Mistakes to avoid in marriage*
Finally, avoid two things in your marriage. First, avoid doing anything ahead of God's timing. Brother, you cannot not run ahead of Him who is carrying you. Second, avoid the spirit of anger and its manifestation inwardly or outwardly as it is one reason for the termination of destiny. The spirit of anger was real and bad in my forefather Levi such that Papa Jacob cursed this spirit of anger. You need to bring to the Lord whatever weakness, sickness or failure that has run in your family for generations. You need to know that these have been nailed to the cross and you have the victory. You have got to be aware that you are at the peak of your success in Christ and therefore you must not allow yourself to be brought down by these shortcomings. In anger, I smote the rock twice instead of speaking to it and God declared that Aaron and I would not physically enter the Promised Land and it was so. My son, may others not reap the reward of your labour of many years as a result of your anger or weakness in Jesus name. You quickly replied with a thunderous "Amen."

### Your rod of authority

We have now walked back to my home and I invited Prophet Moses in for a drink. After we had shared the drink, he gave me the rod in his hand and said: 'The rod is a sign of God's authority over you and your family and on your part a commitment to total submission to His Word, way and will. The word of God in your mouth can be likened to the rod of God in your hand. As from today, in Jesus name, whatever you call forth in faith shall come forth and in line with God's word. The same will happen otherwise to whatever you denounce. Son, choose to speak life, victory, success, healing, godly wealth in your family home, in your marriage and other social world. Choose to speak in Jesus name, permanent death to sickness, afflictions, anger and whatever is trying to limit you or terminate your life or family untimely.

When God called me all I had was the rod in my hand. Son what is your own rod? You need to identify it first. Whether it is your pen, computer, drawings, designs, verbal expression or hospitality. Whatever it is, if you will give it to God, you will be amazed as He turns it into His own blessings for you, your family and community and also an instrument of warfare against your enemies.

*Prophet Moses ended by praying with me saying:*
*Dear Father and our Greatest Shepherd, we come with our hearts of thanksgiving for such a time like this bringing before You ----------(insert your name). Thank You God for leading him in life thus far. As he embarks on the journey of getting married,*

*please give him a humble, teachable spirit; grant that he might have a peaceful and rewarding experience with his in-laws. Father help him and his wife to raise their children in Your love and the truth of Your Word. Help him and his wife also to train their children about the good things in their roots and culture. May ---- (insert your name) never start his life assignment ahead of Your timing and place in Jesus name. As he turns his own rod over to You Father (name it) may it become God's own instrument in his hands with which he will use to establish Your kingdom here on earth and bring direction and leadership to him and his entire household. May his calling be enhanced with his marriage and together with his wife run the race that You have set before them successfully in Jesus name we pray and with thanksgiving. Amen.*

### *Reflections*

I saw Prophet Moses to the door thanking him for his visit and with the rod that he gave me in my hand, I begin to recount all that he said to me that:

- I should be ready to leave my parents and be united with my wife.
- I must avoid starting my life assignment ahead of God's timing and place in Jesus name.
- I should give a lending hand to others whenever and wherever possible in spite of my own current challenges.
- Should I have to live with my in-laws, I should be humble, grateful for their generosity and not abuse the opportunity.
- I should in every way possible give a helping hand to my in-laws and take up my full responsibility as a husband and father.

- I should teach my wife about my godly root and faith.
- Together with my wife we should raise godly children by teaching them God's Word, how to honour Him and about good values in their roots including the good culture, language and food.
- I should have a good relationship with my in-laws.
- Life is often in stages and I need God's presence at every stage of my life.
- I cannot run faster than God who is carrying me and all that concerns me.
- I should identify my own rod and submit it to God to use.
- With God's anointing on my rod and in obedience to His leading and commands, victory is secured for my family and I in Jesus name.
- I should try to avoid being angry as it can be dangerous and catastrophic to my life's assignment.
- I need to address every generational curse, weakness or disease in the name of the Lord so that it does not derail me at the peak of my success.

*The Exposing Lover*

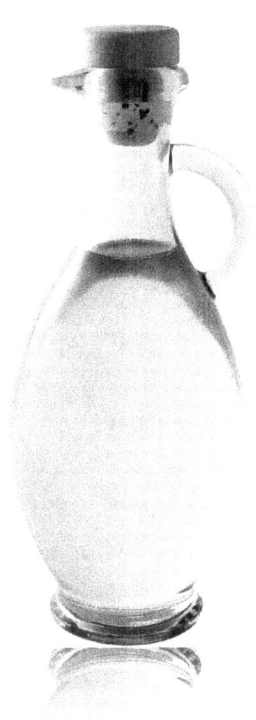

*You anoint my head with oil: my cup overflows. Psalm 23:5 (NIV)*

# The Exposing Lover

*Providing for your family is a command not an option or suggestion.*

*A borrower is always at the mercy of his lenders.*

Your walk in the past three days with great men who have voluntarily re-opened their past and matrimonial lives to you has been full of many 'wow' moments. With greater excitement you are ready much earlier today for your next guest. Just at the right time, you hear a knock on the door. He is fairly younger than your earlier guests but he is dressed as a priest or a prophet. You greet your guest and together, both of you take another route for your evening walk. He begins by saying:

**'In this same way, husbands ought to love their wives as their own bodies. He who loves his wife loves himself' (Ephesians 5: 28. NIV).**

To love is a command not a suggestion or advice. It is imperative to love. Whilst to most women, love is part of their make-up, something that flows from within, almost seamlessly or effortlessly for many men love is an act to be consciously learned

## The Exposing Lover

and expressed. Eve being made from a rib close to Adam's heart is an indication that she is to be treated with respect and love. She is not to be trampled upon or walked over or for her to rule over you as her husband. Let your love for your wife be genuine; giving to her generously, within your means and as often as you can afford. Avoid confusing the desire for self-satisfaction in sexual intercourse to sincere, kind hearted and unconditional love.

* *Try and be practical and real in expressing your love language to your wife.*
* *To read or learn more about the 5 love languages, visit www.5lovelanguages.com or Google - Dr Gary Chapman's love language book.*

You need to love your wife as your body. To show appreciation for your mortal body, you need to give it good and regular treatment, paying attention to what you feed your body – physically, spiritually, in exercise, in the quality of bathing or showering and the quality of rest, food, water and leisure times. Indeed anyone who loves his wife loves his body, for in marriage they are no longer two but one flesh. So, what affects one affects the other.

However it not unusual to find some people who don't know how to love themselves and are therefore unable to pass the same love and affection to their spouses. Love as mentioned earlier can be learned and expressed appropriately. There is so much to godly love that you can read about in 1 Corinthians Chapter 13.

### Now to my story...

I was simply referred to as a man of God and one of the unnamed prophets in the Bible. I served faithfully under one of the greatest prophets at that time and in history – Prophet Elisha. When I became ill and ran into financial difficulties, I took a loan, and believing that it will not get that bad, I used our two sons as collaterals. Whilst I was well known by the great Prophet of God, I did not consult him with my health or financial issues. Looking back now, I sometimes think God perhaps would have used the prophet to resolve both problems. I lived within the territory of abundance yet subsisted on very little as a deplorable pauper suffering bouts of ailments. My refusal to expose my problems in the right circle just compounded my unfortunate circumstances. When I least expected, I returned to our Maker leaving behind an extremely vulnerable widow and children whose destiny I had thoughtlessly consigned to interminable slavery.

### Seek divine counsel

There is an African adage that says 'Concealed problems kill whilst exposed problems flee'. A problem shared is a problem half-solved. In any and every marriage, there will be problems and challenges to various degrees and at various times. The challenges may be financial, social, health, family, wealth, relationship and so on. Don't attempt to bottle the problem or keep it to yourself. Prayerfully and appropriately share it with your wife and godly experts.

Brother, I tell you, just as wise men still seek after Jesus, wise men do seek and go for godly counsel. It is pride and arrogance to think that as a husband and father, you alone should be the 'Think tank' of your family or that it is belittling for you as a man to seek advice or conclude on matters that concern your wife as "That's a woman thing!"

I was called a man of God and servant of God. Brother who are you, and what will you be called now or later?

### *Have a financial mentor and get moneywise*
In what ways are you experiencing indebtedness? Who are you owing and why? The bank or the loan giver will only remain your friend for as long as you keep within the terms of the repayment, not going over even by a day, and for as long as they can make some good profits from you. Do you jump at having all sorts of credit cards or loan offers? Do you spend more than your monthly income? Do you spend all your regular monthly income without having a reasonable savings? If that is the case, you might be positioning yourself for financial indebtedness. Not only is it important for a wise man to have a spiritual mentor, it is equally good for a wise man to have a financial mentor, one who is financially stable and with a growing income greater than expenditure. It is nice to be disciplined and have self-control across board including in how you manage your finances.

If you are already in debt, you need to confirm it, identify why you are into debt and confront it with plans of how to get out and stay free. You and I are not sent to the world to carry the world's financial burden. We must each prayerfully ask the Lord to show and direct us to who in particularly we can help and for how long.

In obtaining any loans either from the banks, financial institutions or wealthy individuals, they often ask for a guarantor or collaterals just in case the person fails to pay up or die before completing the loan payment. In my case I used our two young sons as collaterals, mortgaging their future without their consent!

Brother, what have you used as collaterals for the loan you took or about to take? Which of your family members will negatively be affected by the debt?

*Avoid poverty now and in your marriage. It is more damaging than many other problems. What are you currently doing that might bring poverty into your marriage now or later? Are you an over-spender- spending first and thinking later? Are you lazy, always depending on 'hand-me-downs' from others? Are you experiencing poor health? In which areas are you poor that might affect your family now or later? It is time you addressed the enemy of poverty before it destroys you, your marriage and family.

I returned to our Maker without leaving my wife and children a will or life insurance. I exposed my wife and boys to the merciless debt collectors. The Bible says: "A good father leaves inheritance for his grandchildren (Proverbs 13:22); meaning that as a good father, you should leave your immediate children and grandchildren good inheritance that will start them off positively in life. Please avoid subjecting your wife and household to heartless debt collectors. How well have you prepared for your wife's financial needs or your children's educational fees? There are various suitable bank savings account options you can choose from for your needs and pocket.

Taking a life insurance for yourself and wife is not evil thinking but forward planning for no one knows when their Maker would call for them. I didn't know when either. What if He calls you in the prime of your life, what if He calls you when you least expected? What if He calls you home ahead of your wife? How would you expect your wife, children and relatives to cope? Unless you are able to leave your wife and children a big pot of wealth, they are likely to suffer when you are gone. The alternative is to prayerfully consider taking a life insurance that your family can fall back on.

Writing a will may be the next important document you consider in your marriage after your marriage certificate. In some cultures, once the father passes on to glory, the man's family are at liberty to raid his home and take whatever they want without due consideration for his wife and children. In some cruel situations, the widow and children are forced out of the home without allowing them to take with them as much as a pin! They would say that the properties belong to the dead man, which may not be entirely true. Generally speaking, it is unlikely that his widow came into the marriage empty-handed and had not contributed anything into the family since they married. She most unlikely would have been a silent partner in the relationship. Neither would she be one bereft of ideas that would enhance and promote a positive image and the success of her family. Brother, please protect your wife and children by having a well written will to cover all aspects of your wife's and children's welfare, education, spiritual and financial wellbeing. Please avoid exposing your wife and innocent children to bailiffs, debt collectors, molesters, and opportunists who might want to harass or molest them when you are no more.

### *Identify your potentials and assets*
\*The most painful part of my story is that I returned to our Maker or simply put died without realising that the key to terminate my family's poverty and indebtedness was within my home, my wife and a bottle of oil! The bottle of oil was there in our home all the time and yet I did not realise that my family's financial breakthrough was in it. I did not think much of the oil or seek the face of the Lord for the way out of debt. My son, I can guarantee you that the key to your financial breakthrough is within your home if you will take time to prayerfully ask God to show it to you. It may be a recipe for food or medicine or drink, which your parents or grandparents passed down to you. It may be an item of furniture, farmland, or a trade that you have grown too familiar with all these years. It might even be a talent or skill or gifting that you have taken for granted, for example your baritone voice. As you seek the face of the Lord and godly counsel, remember to carry along your wife and children too.

---

\* *There is more on the exposition of this in the 'Enemy Within' by Oluwakemi Ola-Ojo. ISBN 978-1-908-015-11-2 Check it out @ www.amazon.co.uk/com.*

*The Exposing Lover*

Your wife may not be half as gifted or educated or exposed or knowledgeable or strong as you but please carry her along all the same.

Thankfully, my wife sought for help from Prophet Elisha. She identified what we had in the house, took instructions from the man of God, obeyed it to the letters, and bang, came the financial breakthrough for the loan repayment and financial provision for the rest of their lives. Brother, please carry your wife and children along in every situation you might encounter in your marriage. Seek for spiritual and financial guidance. Don't die prematurely and don't die poor.

### *Make the most of your opportunities*
Whilst it is good to serve in the church and ministry, don't get too engrossed in helping and resolving issues in the lives of others that you neglect talking to someone else about the challenges you face. You as a man should not hide your problems from your pastor, prophet or spiritual oversight. Brother, identify the grace and the anointing of the man of God where you worship. Only the anointing you tap into will work for you. My master, Prophet Elisha, was a man of unusual anointing, doubling the miracles of his predecessor, Prophet Elijah. I worked faithfully with him but did not ask for help regarding my health issues or indebtedness. 'Ask and it shall be given' the Bible says but I failed to ask the man of God for help in my times of need.

---
\* For a full read turn to 2 Kings 4:1-8.
\* There is more on the exposition of this under God's Provision – My Part in 'Good Mums, Bad Mums' by Oluwakemi Ola-Ojo. ISBN 978-0-9557898-1-6
Check it out @ www.amazon.co.uk/com.

Looking back now, how I wish I had asked. When the axe head fell, my colleague asked and shouted for help and Prophet Elisha performed an unparalleled miracle, even till today. 2 Kings 6:1-7. When my widow wife later asked for help, Prophet Elisha told her what to do to get out of indebtedness and live wealthy for the rest of my family's life. Prophet Elisha's dead bones even had enough anointing to raise the dead that was how much of God's anointing that was with and in him! 2 Kings 13:20-21. Brother, don't just serve faithfully but tap into the anointing by asking. Learn to ask God and learn to ask those around you. Don't be proud or shy or too busy or too faithful to ask. It's not only a woman's thing to ask. Asking for help belittles no one especially at crucial times in life. If one person turns you down, God will lead you to the one who will assist you. You might want to read 2Kings 4 :1-7, 6 :1-7, Luke 15:1-32, John 15:7, 16:23-24 and Matthew 7:7-11.

The church should be a place of worship, service and ministering to your own personal need. It is not a sin neither is it unmanly to have life challenges. It is common but less talked about in the church even in some of the men's ministry but nevertheless my brother, don't hide your problems from the right people who can help you. The Church has been likened to the hospital where we go to seek for healing where and when it hurts.

Identify the talents, skills and experiences of your boss and colleagues where you do your secular job and tap into them. Someone has been where you are trying to go or has achieved what you are aspiring to become. If God grants you the opportunity to be around such people, make the best use of such a privilege and do not abuse such an advantage either. Serve faithfully but call for help when and where needed.

Brother, daily identify opportunities and tap into them. Opportunities of information that could help you, of people that you meet who could point you in the right direction to where you are going or need to be; opportunities of more education or wisdom in your chosen field or career. Remember always you are 'captain' over God's inheritance. 1 Samuel 9 – 10;1. Many are poor or unfulfilled, in the wrong career or profession as they refuse to identify and use their daily God-sent opportunities. May your story not be like that in Jesus' name.

The oil in the bottle was probably at home during the crisis that led to my death but I ignored it. Oil was a basic essential in the house. I did not value or considered it. Often times our solution lies in what we sometimes disregard.

Prayerfully make use of your accesses and the windows of opportunities that come your way especially if you need them. It may even be just asking questions that will point you in the right direction, provide solution to your problem. I was one of the sons of the prophet who had access to Elisha the prophet but I did not involve him in my health or financial issues. I should have cried like the other son who shouted when the axe head fell in the water.

* *There is more on the exposition of this in the 'Enemy Within' by Oluwakemi Ola-Ojo. ISBN 978-1-908-015-11-2 Check it out @ www.amazon.co.uk/com.*

*To the Groom with Love*

You are now both back to your door from the walk. You politely ask this unnamed prophet in for a drink, after which he gave you a small bottle of olive oil and proceeds to pray saying:

Dear Lord and Father, it is with a heart of gratitude that we have come to You for such a time as this. Thank You Father for granting me the opportunity of sharing with Your son -----------*(insert your name)*. As he goes into this marriage, please grant him the wisdom and ability to stay away from all forms of indebtedness and disease. Help him O Lord in humility to seek for godly counsel in every area of need. May he honestly be open with his wife in their relationship. Father help him to be wise and provide for him in abundance that he will leave a good inheritance for his children and grandchildren in Jesus name. O Lord open his eyes to see Your provision for every need in his home and marriage. Oil is for anointing and oil brings ease and cooking oil provides flavor to the food, my Father, I pray that Your anointing will rest on Your son------, may he achieve his goals with ease and may his life be flavoured by Your Holy Spirit. May he not die prematurely or die poor. In Jesus name we have prayed with thanksgiving. Amen.

### *Reflections*

You thanked the unnamed prophet and saw him to the door. With the bottle of oil in your hand you start to recap your discussion:

- I must learn to love my wife as my body for in marriage both are one flesh.

- I should seek for godly counsel in every area of our family need.
- I should have open communication with my wife.
- I should avoid all forms of indebtedness and poverty in my marriage.
- I should not be shy or proud to ask for help from the right quarters or circle.
- I must have a financial mentor.
- It is reasonable and sensible to have a life insurance, have and leave a will for my family.
- I should avoid using any of my family members as collaterals for my loans, and avoid sending my children or wife into slavery.
- For every need that comes up after our marriage, God has His provision right within my home if I care to seek for godly counsel.

*"What an exposition!" You mumble as you meditate and you are off to sleep.*

*Looking unto Jesus, the author and finisher of our faith. Hebrews 12:2 (NKJV)*

# The God Fearing Lover

*Character is better than beauty any day!*

Even though this will be your fifth evening walk, your mind is still much open and excited as you prepare for tonight's walk with your guest. Just as you are ready, there comes the expected knock on the door. You open the door and see a fairly middle aged immaculately dressed man in military uniform with an Army General star on his uniform. Without thinking you salute this officer and he politely returns the salute. He then says, 'at ease' and holds your hand leading the way using another route for your walk.

He begins his talk by saying:
**'A wife of noble character is her husband's crown, but a disgraceful wife is like decay in his bones' (Proverbs 12:4).**

Brother please be careful who you marry. It is pleasing to marry a physically beautiful and attractive wife of your taste, however, of greater importance is to marry a woman of a noble character; a woman of virtue and high moral principles. Beauty, with time, in both the groom and bride may fail but a noble character just gets better by the day. A woman with integrity is much better any day. There is something about the inner beauty of a woman that by far outweighs the physical one.

### Now to my story...

I am Uriah, a top-ranking officer in King David's army. As a committed top military officer, I defended our nation, the King and the Ark of the Covenant with my life. I was a trustworthy officer who carried out the king's order to the letter. Brother, it is nice to have good works ethics.

By virtue of my job, my wife Bathsheba and I lived not too far from my boss, King David – a great man and excellent soldier himself. In my days, bathrooms were outside of the house and with no roof. Just like today, military officers don't go to war with their wives or children. Once during a military assignment, King David was at home relaxing. One evening whilst walking on his house roof, he saw my beautiful wife having a shower. He immediately sent for her. The woman I had trusted and loved found it difficult to resist my boss's flattering, flirty advances and promiscuous indulgences. She was beautiful but like a reed somewhat easy to sway.. Whilst I was in the cold, often hungry, putting my life on the line for my boss and wife, both were wantonly engaged in licentious lust somewhere in the palace! On second thought, in fairness to Bathsheba, it was perhaps not easy to turn down the advances of the king of the realm when he called for her even though he already had several wives and concubines!

## To the Groom with Love

Brother, try not to expose your wife to men who are wolves who will take advantage of your momentary absence to take over your place in the heart and life of your wife. Avoid anything that might lead your wife to being exposed to heartless and wicked men including some so-called men of God. Be very mindful of whom you expose your wife to. Be aware of her vulnerabilities and keep her out of harm's way.

It is not unusual for beautiful women to be chased or visited by their husband's employer, superior, closest friends, relative and some so-called men of God when the husband is not around especially when the woman feels very vulnerable. Who can you trust to look in on your wife in your absence.Is your wife of a noble character who will keep herself only for you when you are not there?

Unknown to me, my wife got pregnant for my boss and the king planned a way to get rid of me. The king suddenly sent for me from the battlefield and I could not understand why. The king after hearing about the situation on the battlefield sent me home, hoping that I would then make love to my wife. The king had forgotten we had been trained to avoid sexual affairs when preparing for or at war. To avoid the temptation, I slept with the king's guards in the palace that night. The second day the king got his servants to get me drunk but even so I would not lower my guard in righteousness. Looking back now I can see how the king made extensive effort to lure me to go home to my wife.

Finally the king released me to go back to the battlefield but gave me a letter to deliver to my army commander. This I did, not knowing that it was my own death warrant for an offence that I did not commit. I was set up for a bloody death just because of my beautiful wife and the unplanned pregnancy.

### *Uriah's Prayer*

You had now reached your home and you ask General Uriah in for a drink. Just as he is leaving he gives you a badge that reads 'In the Lord's army' and prays saying:

> *Father in the name of Jesus Christ have we come to You today, first to thank You for Your mercies endures forever. Lord we are grateful for our lives to this point. Father, I thank You for Your son ----- -------- (please insert your name ). Grant him Your divine favour so that he might choose a woman of noble character in Jesus name. Help him to be diligent at what he does. Help him not to expose his wife to heartless men inadvertently whoever they are as he goes about his business as the breadwinner for his family. Lord, please give him the spirit of discernment to understand the terms of his contract and assignment. May his life not be cut short untimely by those who want to take over his wife. Lord, please fight all his battles for him and his family from now in Jesus name we have prayed with thanksgiving. Amen.*

## *To the Groom with Love*

### *Reflections*

As General Uriah leaves with his gift in my hand, I begin to recall what he told me that:

- I should prayerfully marry a woman of a noble character.
- I should be God-fearing and have good work ethics.
- I should avoid living where my wife and family will be exposed to sexual harassment or abuse.
- It is not unusual for beautiful women to be chased or visited by their husband's employer, superior, closest friends, and relative when the husband is not around especially when the woman feels very vulnerable.
- I need to think about whom to trust to look after my wife in my absence. (Should I by the nature of my work travel periodically.)
- I should learn to prayerfully read the lines and between the lines of the contract of my assignment etc.

## THE TEN COMMANDMENTS

1. I AM THE LORD YOUR GOD. YOU SHALL WORSHIP THE LORD YOUR GOD AND HIM ONLY SHALL YOU SERVE.

2. YOU SHALL NOT TAKE THE NAME OF THE LORD YOUR GOD IN VAIN.

3. REMEMBER TO KEEP HOLY THE SABBATH DAY.

4. HONOR YOUR FATHER AND YOUR MOTHER.

5. YOU SHALL NOT KILL.

6. YOU SHALL NOT COMMIT ADULTERY.

7. YOU SHALL NOT STEAL.

8. YOU SHALL NOT BEAR FALSE WITNESS.

9. YOU SHALL NOT COVET YOUR NEIGHBOR'S WIFE.

10. YOU SHALL NOT COVET YOUR NEIGHBOR'S GOODS.

*Let it be the hidden person of the heart, with the incorruptible beauty of a gentle and quiet spirit, which is very precious in the sight of God*
*1st Peter 3:4 (NKJV)*

# The Unwary Lover.

*Disobedience will always take one back to where one does not want to be.*

*Disobedience often leads to isolation from loved ones and loved places.*

Today marks Day 6 of your evening walk with various guests who have gone the way you are about to walk in life. You are nicely dressed and ready. Just then you hear the knock at the door. You open the door and see a middle-aged man with a neat dreadlock hairstyle suggesting he is a Nazarite. Apart from his hairstyle, he looked like any other man on the planet. You are guessing which prophet is this. He seems to be able to read your mind and says, "I am Samson." He asked: "Please, are we ready for our walk," to which you boldly say, "Yes Sir." As you take another route today, He begins by saying:

> **'There is a way that appears to be right, but in the end it leads to death. Proverbs 14:12 and 16:25, Better to live in a desert, than with a quarrelsome and nagging wife. Proverbs 21:19'**

## The Unwary Lover

Brother, in life there are two main ways: the right way and the wrong way. Appearance can be deceiving. Many times, what appears to be right initially leads to nowhere but a dead end. That many people are using a particular way does not guarantee the way to be right or that only a few walk it does not make it wrong either. The rights and wrongs of life can only be determined by the Word of God. It is better to be unpopular but be on God's side than be popular and be on the side of Satan's.

Everyone needs peace especially at home. One of the worst things that can happen to a man in marriage is to have a quarrelsome or nagging wife. Do you know what the Bible says about a nagging wife? Let me share some of this with you.

*A foolish son brings disgrace to his father. A nagging wife goes on and on like the drip, drip, drip of the rain. Proverbs 19:13*

*Better to stay outside on the roof of your house than to live inside with a nagging wife. Proverbs 21:9*

*It's better out in the desert than at home with a nagging, complaining wife. Proverbs 21:19*

*It's better to stay outside on the roof of your house than to live inside with a nagging wife. Proverbs 25:24*

*The steady dripping of rain and the nagging of a wife are one and the same. Proverbs 27:15*

*To the Groom with Love*

*It's easier to catch the wind or hold olive oil in your hand than to stop a nagging wife. Proverbs 27:16*

### Now to my story…

I was born to the Manoahs, parents who were once barren. An angel appeared to my mum first when she was in the fields and later to both of my parents and they were told that God was going to bless them with a son. Mum was instructed to not drink any wine or strong drink or eat anything unclean for I was to be a Nazarite from the womb, consecrated unto God. They were told that my life assignment was to deliver my people the Israelites from the hands of the Philistines who had by then oppressed Israel for 40 years.

My brother, (insert your name) you were created for a specific assignment. Prayerfully take time to find it and walk in that divine assignment. Dad and Mum kept to the terms of the instructions, and indeed I was born. I was told about my conception, birth and assignment as often as I can remember whilst growing up. I looked like any other man physically but I carried so much of God's anointing that no man, army or city could stand my physical strength or match my fighting skills. I feared no man for I knew with God in me victory was guaranteed

Your parents may not be as educated or as knowledgeable as you are. Their lifetime income might be less than or equivalent to your daily or weekly allowance. They may not know people outside your village or town or county whilst you may be a world traveller, international executive and a well sought-after figure. But one thing is sure, under normal circumstances, they love you and have your best interest at heart. Nothing enhances or terminates great destinies like the person one is married to. Please prayerfully consider your parents' counsel now and when you have the opportunity to do so.

### *Obedience protects*
By the time I became a man and thought myself ready to marry, I saw a Philistine woman from Timnar and told my parents to get her for me. Dad and Mum tried to counsel me about not marrying from among the uncircumcised but I refused their advice and I made them go down with me to ask for her hand in marriage. Brother, be careful not to try and twist the hands of your parents and force them to go along with your wishes. Remember, a child is to honour his or her parents as that is the first commandment with a reward. With your parents being under pressure and acting in love, you might get your way but remember you will have to live with your choice for life.

On the way to Timnar I killed a young lion that roared against me with my bare hands. Some days later while on the same route, I noted some fresh honey on the dead carcass and I ate some and gave my parents to eat but I did not tell them the source of the honey. Not only had I disobeyed my parents, I defiled myself by eating from a dead animal. In the end my bride was given to another friend.

God's laws, small or big, when obeyed are in our own interest. His love separates us but His laws keep us from known and unknown harm. At another time I spent a whole day laying with a prostitute for twenty-four hours. Brother, God warns us against relationship with the unbeliever. As light and darkness cannot mix, we might think we are winning but this will be short-lived. There is nothing in the camp of the enemy that is worth desiring or accumulating because in the end bitterness and heartaches will be the result.

Looking back now, I had no business with a prostitute as that was an indication of my lack of self-control in the emotional and sexual department. It was a subtle indication of my beginning to pollute my body, which was meant to be God's temple. It is wrong to make love to a woman outside of your marriage bed. A prostitute then, and now, is a sure highway to hell. Also remember that you may contract all manners of sexually transmitted diseases, get blackmailed and become financiallly bankrupt.

That everybody does it today or sleeps around does not make it approved by God or right for you. You were born as a special gift from God to your parents with a definite life assignment for which without your having a genuine and continuous relationship with God cannot fulfill.

### *Identify your strengths and weaknesses*
My urge to settle down like my mates was good and laudable but my thirst for sexual satisfaction in the camp of the enemy was my greatest weakness. I was looking for the right thing in the wrong place, seeking for sexual satisfaction from the wrong

people. I dared going into the enemy's camp to fulfill my lust. With the benefit of hindsight, now I can tell you that only fools and unwise people go to where angels dread.

Have you identified your weakness and what are you doing about it? To whom are you accountable? Who gives you godly counsel on your strengths and weaknesses? Which people's company or environment strengthens your weakness and diminishes your strength and what are you still doing with such people or in such places? Many men have become enslaved once they have slept with the wrong woman. As you heed the warning, may your story not be like it Jesus name.

Then finally I met beautiful Delilah and married her out of lust. Physical beauty and sexual gratification were more important to me and I forgot that she was a woman who neither knew my God, the One and true God, nor have any business obeying or honouring Him. Avoid going into marriage thinking you will change your spouse. My strength was a threat to her instead of being blessing and joy. The call of God on my life was irrelevant and meaningless to her; instead she wanted me devalued, overpowered, demoralized, disabled, destroyed and derailed from my God-assigned mission in life.

### Pitfalls in relationship

To my surprise, all Delilah wanted was to find the source of my strength. I initially lied to her a few times; and each time she had prepared enemies who I single-handedly defeated. Looking back now, I should have walked out of the relationship immediately and kept my life and anointing but I stayed and thought I could handle it with my own strength.

Events in courtship or early in marriage can be pointers to the future of the relationship if not sorted out at the onset or after its first manifestation. Brother, avoid going where angels dare to tread. When you can and are able get yourself out, end such a nagging relationship. Don't be foolhardy enough to put up with such a partner. I ignored every warning sign that was obvious in our marriage then. I did not seek the face of God on how to resolve the issues that were so obvious in this relationship. I neither sought godly counsel of my God-fearing parents nor did I do the easiest thing which would have meant just walking away completely.

### *Uncompromisingly fear God*
The Bible says the heart of man is desperately wicked and corrupt who can know it but God? (Jeremiah 17:9). Never compromise when your life or God-ordained destiny is at stake. Flee if you have to than become enslaved by the enemy. A kiss, a peck, another glass of alcohol or wine, a cigarette or some hard core pornography, a slap on the face, some serious threats or anything that is weakening or devaluing your strength or strengthening your weakness are indicators for you to end the relationship or escape back to your biological or spiritual family. We cannot remain in sin and ask that grace continues to abide with us. When one disobeys God and his parents, if care is not taken,

one is setting oneself up for a life of isolation, loneliness, untold punishment and perhaps untold abuse from one's spouse.

When Delilah realized that I was not going to tell her the secret of my strength, she nagged me every day with her words until I became so sore. One day out of frustration and after she had vexed my soul unto death, I told her the source of my strength. Delilah and her team sprang into action and before I knew it my hair – the symbol of my consecration unto God, the source of my strength and energy - was shaved off. I thought I would jump up as before but now I was helpless and devoid of energy and strength as the Spirit of God had departed.

### *Sin robs you of fellowship with God*
It is the presence of God that makes an ordinary man do extraordinary things for God and His people. The Holy Spirit does not owe anyone a duty to announce His departure. Gradually and over time, my chosen lifestyle was disobeying God, His anointing, His ministry through me and His commandments. Sin will gradually rob a person of their fellowship with God. One's fear and love of God and if care is not taken, the Holy Spirit will depart. I disobeyed my parents and insisted on having my own way. I touched a dead animal and ate from a dead animal. I engaged in illicit affairs with unbelievers who did not share my Jehovah God or fear Him and who did not respect my destiny but wanted my downfall by all means.

Continued disobedience to God, His principles and commandments will grieve the Holy Spirit and make the Holy

## The Unwary Lover

Spirit leave a person without warning and or the person's knowledge. It is a terrible thing to be devoid of the presence and personality of the Holy Spirit. No wonder King David cried in Psalms 51:10-12 saying "Cast me not away from Your presence Oh Lord, take not thy Holy Spirit from me, restore unto me the joy of thy salvation and renew a right spirit within me." Brother, sin will rob anyone of their strength and a person without strength is as helpless as a doll; subject to being thrown around, messed up and devalued by satanic forces.

The weaknesses of great men that were not overcome brought them down. I was specially anointed to be a judge and deliverer but my lust for strange women reduced me to a blind man overnight. King David's affair introduced the sword into his household. King Solomon later worshipped idols in his old age instead of the true God because of the foreign women he married. Brother, identify your weakness and prayerfully work on it. Have godly mentors who are strong in your areas of weakness, and in humility, listen and use their advice so that you can fulfill God's plan for your life.

I was robbed of my source of power and anointing before my eyes were gouged out. The physical pain and shock cannot be imagined, I was ridiculed, mugged, mocked and forced to grind in the prison. All these happened to me with Delilah's approval and her teaming up with my enemies. She did not protest against my ordeal as she had been paid to betray me. Then it became very clear that by marrying Delilah I had isolated myself from my parents and family and from God and my calling. I prematurely terminated my God-given assignment, and the worst part was that I had married an enemy.

I was made to dance before the Philistines' gods. There in the house of their gods, I prayed to the Almighty God and asked Him to help me. Though God helped me, I died a shameful, painful and childless death.

Brother, by all means avoid any woman who will keep you isolated from your family and godly friends, or from God and His calling over your life however beautiful she may look. One of Satan's tricks up till now and forever is to isolate God's own anointed before destroying such a person. Learn from me son, disobedience to God or one's parents often births heartaches and premature death if care is not taken.

By now you had both got back to your house and you shared a drink with Judge Samson. He gave you a copy of the Ten Commandments (Exodus 20) and the summarised two commandments of Jesus, which are first to love the Lord your God with all of your being and love your neighbor as yourself (Matt 22:37-40, Mark 12:30-31). He leads in prayer for you saying:

> *Dear Father and Lord of all mankind please forgive us our foolish ways and re-clothe us in Your rightful mind. Father we thank You for Your son ------(insert your name) who is trying to get married. Lord, I pray that he will honour and not disobey his parents in his choice. May he never be married to an*

*unbeliever or enemy however beautiful the woman may look. Father, Son and the Holy Spirit, help him not to marry an anointing or purpose destroyer. May he not toy with Your anointing that is upon his life and may he be wise and have Your discernment to know what to do with nagging people or satanic situations that may want to destroy him in Jesus name. Finally, may he not die a shameful, painful, childless or premature death in Jesus name we pray with thanksgiving. Amen.*

### *Reflections*

You thank Pa Samson and see him off to the door. As you prepare for bed later that evening you continue to ponder on what Pa Samson told you that:

- As a child of God, I have been created for a specific purpose in life.
- I should find God's purpose for my life. In doing this I might need to ask my biological parents (if they are alive and they know it).
- I should honour God and my parents in my choice of a wife. I should not disregard my parent's advice and counsel.
- I should avoid disobeying my parents in whom I choose to marry.
- I must avoid everything that will defile my body, spirit and soul.
- I should avoid marrying an unbeliever.

## The Unwary Lover

- I must not marry from the enemy's camp.
- Isolation by spouse from my family and long trusted friends may be indicative of an impending danger or trouble.
- I should avoid tossing my anointing before my enemies.
- Should I find that I have married an enemy, I should prayerfully seek godly counsel on what to do.
- I should not toy with God's anointing that is upon my life or compromise my walk with and for Him.
- Every gift and talent must be given back to God to use in and through me and I must have a grateful attitude.
- I must prayerfully avoid a shameful premature and painful death.

*I have hidden Your word in my heart, that I may not sin against You. Psalm 119: 11 (NIV)*

# The Redeeming Lover

*True love forgives and forgets all wrongs.*

The past six days have been filled with encounters with great men from the Bible who had kindly visited you and shared their life experiences. Yet you are still excited to meet your final guest. You are ready and just then, there is a knock on the door. Your final guest is dressed as a prophet and you are wondering who among the prophets this is. As you both start your walk, your guest says, "I am Prophet Hosea"

*'Husbands love your wives, just as Christ loved the church and gave himself up for her. Ephesians 5:25 NIV'.*

The above scripture to the man is a command and not a suggestion or advice. Love for some men is to be learned and rightfully expressed. Loving one's wife is likened to Jesus Christ's sacrificial and unconditional love for the Church. True love is about giving and sharing selflessly.

**Now to my story...**
I am one of the prophets in the Bible. As a prophet of God, certain characteristics are expected of me in my calling. However

our Sovereign God is full of surprises. God spoke and instructed me to go and marry a prostitute and have children with her! My marriage was based on God's leading. God is able to and will give you divine instructions in your marriage. You, however, need to know God personally for yourself. Be familiar with how He speaks to you and be prepared to obey Him at all times. God's revelation needs no second opinion.

Though the office of the priests and the prophets are not exactly the same, they are in some respects very similar. The Bible clearly defines the type of person the high priest can marry. The woman he marries must be a virgin and not a widow, not a divorced woman or a woman defiled by prostitution, but only a virgin from his own people (Leviticus 21: 7, 13- 14, Ezekiel 44:22)

Ordinarily all considerations that accompany getting married can be tough and challenging but marrying a professional prostitute was quite daunting for me. Nonetheless, I was not going to go against it having heard clearly from God. Brother, may the Lord grant you the ability to hear Him personally and always, and the grace to obey Him in Jesus name. Amen.

Many men look for the physically attractive to marry and few will naturally want to marry someone who has undeniable physical, financial or social challenges for obvious reasons. What if God tells you to marry such a woman who has a baggage of challenges? What will you do? God's love through you can make a remarkable difference and bring the best out of such relationships.

Though I was married to Gomer, she left after having four children for me and returned into prostitution. Yet again God instructed me to bail my wife Gomer out from her new lover. First, I married her based on God's leading. Second, in accordance with God's instructions, I redeemed her from her new lover for fifteen shekels of silver and about a homer and a lethek of barley. The Grace of God will always seek the sinner to redeem even at the cost of Jesus' death on the cross.

God used the names of our children and Gomer's unfaithfulness to speak to Israel and Judah. Don't be surprised should God choose to use your marriage to speak to your family, friends, community and nation.

Equally together with your wife, be prayerful and be careful with the choice of names you give to your children. Will they be names that will honour God; for example Noah - He will comfort us in the labour and painful toil of our hands caused by the ground the Lord has cursed (Genesis 5: 28 – 29) or Isaac – laughter (Genesis 21:1-6), or names that will dishonor God or cause heartaches to the child in life? Three examples of such names were Nabal – foolish (1 Samuel 25: 23-25), Jabez – sorrow (2 Chronicles 4:9), Ichabod -the glory has departed from Israel, for the ark of God has been captured.

My wife Gomer was addicted to prostitution, which she needed help for. Be aware that you may soon find some ungodly habits in your wife that will need God's redemption through you. Brother should your wife need such help, what price are you willing to pay to redeem her from all unhealthy habits, sickness, poverty, ignorance, and financial, emotional, spiritual or physical oppression? Challenging and shameful as this task might be, God is able to bring deliverance to your wife and family through you in Jesus name. Amen.

My marriage to Gomer was challenging as we both came from totally and completely opposite backgrounds. Our aspirations, the types of friends we keep, value system, etc. were very different. For any marriage to succeed both parties must strive to make it work but in our case much more was required from me. I could have given up if I did not hear from God but I did hear God ask me to marry her.

It is good to serve God but my brother should you find that your wife or child needs help with some physical, emotional, spiritual, financial or sexual challenges, find time to attend to such needs and avoid using your service in the house of God as a cover up for not being there for her or the child.

God granted me the grace for long suffering so I could accommodate the weaknesses of my wife and her periodical absence from home and her escape to her former lifestyle. Our God is long suffering, He loves the sinner but hates the sin and would always go the extra mile to redeem the sinner.

*To the Groom with Love*

Prophet Hosea ended his talk by saying:
*Who is wise? Let them realize these things. Who is discerning? Let them understand. The ways of the Lord are right; the righteous walk in them, but the rebellious stumble in them.*

By now you are both back and you offer Prophet Hosea a drink, which he accepts. He hands you a Bible as your gift and pray saying:

*Our Father and Lord, what a great privilege that I have to be chosen to share this precious moment with Your son ----------------(please insert your name). Please my Father help him to know You personally, hear You clearly and obey You willingly. Grant him all that he might need should he have to rescue his wife and family from all unhealthy habits, sickness, poverty, ignorance, and financial, emotional, spiritual oppression. In Jesus name we pray with thanksgiving. Amen. And now may:*

*'The Lord bless you and keep you;
The Lord make His face shine upon you,
And be gracious to you;
The Lord lift up His countenance upon you,
And give you peace in Jesus name.' Amen*

### *Reflections*

You thank Prophet Hosea and see him off to the door.
'Whoa' you say. Short, precise but equally loaded; and you quickly begin to recollect what you have been told as:

- ♦ I must learn to hear God clearly and obey Him

- I should marry based on God's leading.
- Loving my wife is a command by God not a suggestion or advice.
- It is possible for me to learn to love and express love to my wife.
- God is very much able to bless our marriage with children in spite of all odds.
- I must give God-glorifying names to our children.
- God can use our marriage and children's names to speak volumes to us, our community and nation.
- I must learn to have quality 'us' time with my wife in order to bridge the gap in communication and to have a better understanding of each other.
- I must learn to accommodate my wife's weaknesses and foibles knowing that God ordained our relationship.
- With God's help, I should be prepared for whatever it will take to redeem my wife and family from every unhealthy habit, sickness, poverty, ignorance, financial, emotional and spiritual oppression.

You immediately fall on your knees in worship, adoration and prayers to our Lord and Maker for the visits from these seven heroes, for the clarity of how to find a godly wife, and for knowing what your role will be after you exchange the marriage vows.

# POEMS

## HAVE YOU GOTTEN TO THE WELL?

*Abraham household administrator travelled*
*On a journey to go and get a wife for Isaac*
*A difficult assignment it seemed to him*
*Arriving at the outskirts of Iraq*
*He stood beside the well and prayed to Jehovah*
*And there he met Rebekah who later married Isaac.*

*Jacob running away from Esau to Haran*
*Got to the well and saw flocks to be watered*
*Waiting there Rachel came with her flock*
*She was shapely and in every way a beauty*
*No wonder Jacob instantly fell in love with her*
*He worked for Laban for fourteen years to get her.*

*Beloved Joseph the dreamer was Jacob's old age son*
*In God's love he was shown his own future*
*Out of jealousy and hatred his own brothers*
*Threw him into a dry well alive and later sold him.*
*To the Midianites who sold him to Potiphar in Egypt*
*And finally he rose to become Egypt's sole administrator.*

## To the Groom with Love

*Moses, afraid of Pharaoh, ran to the land of Midian*
*Sitting beside a well, Jethro's seven daughters came*
*To draw water and fill the water trough for the flock*
*Moses rescued them from the other shepherds and helped*
*Later he was invited by Jethro to live with him.*
*And married Zipporah, one of the ladies he met at the well.*

*Around noon on the way to Sychar village*
*Jesus stopped beside Jacob's well and alone he was*
*His disciples were away to the village to buy some food*
*There came a despised Samaritan woman at the well*
*She wanted to fetch well water but later got the living water.*
*From Jesus who told her history and answered her questions.*

*My brother, my sister. Have you gotten to the well?*
*As you face that difficult assignment like Abrahams' servant*
*As you face your fear and frustration through life*
*As you have been thrown into the dry well of life*
*As you with your load of sin and guilt go about*
*\*For at the well, Jesus is waiting to meet your need!*

*Genesis 24:1-67, 29:1-30, 37:1-36, Exodus 2:1-2, \*John 4:1-41.*

*To the Groom with Love*

# WHERE DO YOU PICK YOUR CHOICE?

*In a man's life he is bound to make some choices*
*The choice of where to live, what to do and what to eat*
*The choice of where to work and who to have as friends*
*The choice of what to wear and how to dress up.*

*Among these numerous decisions and options to choose from*
*The choice of a life partner is very significant*
*For the two shall no longer be separate but one*
*One in body, thinking, action, and in their decisions.*

*Where do you pick your choice my brother, my sister?*
*From the beer parlour, hotel or wild night party?*
*From your working place, neighbourhood or village?*
*From your church or your fellowship?*

*Where you pick your choice from is very important*
*Isaac and Jacob's choices were from their tribe*
*Samson the anointed was from the heathen*
*That was the beginning of his trouble and death.*

*David and Solomon's choices of marrying women*
*From many of the heathen tribes created problems*
*That of undisciplined children and rebellion against them*
*In their old age these women turned their hearts away from God.*

*To the Groom with Love*

*For you to make the right choice of a life partner*
*You need to have Jesus Christ living in you*
*Where is the man that fears the Lord.*
*The Lord will help him to choose the best.*

*The priests were a chosen group among the tribes*
*But for them to remain in the service of the Lord*
*There was a rule of marrying only from their tribe*
*For they must not profane their offspring among their people*

*For you are chosen generation, a royal priesthood*
*Called by God, sanctified and set apart for Him*
*Do not be unequally yoked with unbelievers*
*For what has light got to do with darkness?*

*Matthew 19:5-6, Proverbs 2:9 Leviticus 2:7-14 &15,20: and Deuteronomy 7:6*

## ALONE WITH GOD

*Many of us want to hear from God,*
*To listen to His small still voice,*
*Yet we never provide such an atmosphere,*
*And might not be quiet in our spirit,*
*To get directives and instructions from Him.*

*Jacob, frightened to meet Esau,*
*On his way back home as directed by God,*
*With two armies and many flock,*
*Got assurance from God after wrestling with the angel,*
*While alone on the other side of River Jordan.*

*Great men and women in the Bible,*
*Became great for they heard from God,*
*Whilst they were alone with Him,*
*They found time out of none to be with their Maker,*
*In prayers and the study of His Word.*

*Many of us complain of our busy schedule,*
*For some it's their children, their family or their wealth,*
*Whilst for others it's their many responsibilities,*
*Even when alone in their closets at home,*
*Their minds are not quieted to hear God.*

*To the Groom with Love*

*Alone with God my brother,*
*Get your spirit off your family and associates,*
*Off your many duties and responsibilities,*
*In the closet of your heart talk with God,*
*In prayers and meditation on God's Words.*

*Time spent alone with God in your closet,*
*Is time better spent than any other time,*
*For not only will you be reassured,*
*Comforted, encouraged and nurtured,*
*It is a time of receiving clear directives from God.*

*Take time to be alone with God my brother, my friend,*
*Wherever you are now and whatever you may be doing,*
*God is ready to give you directives on your problems,*
*For 'in returning and rest you shall be saved,*
*In quietness and in trust shall be your strength'.*

*Genesis 22:9-12, 22-32 & Isaiah 30:15.*

## OPPORTUNITY TO BECOME A CHRISTIAN

*Dear Father in heaven,*

*Thank you for the privilege of reading this book. 'Indeed I have sinned and come short of Your glory.' I am grateful to You for sending Jesus Christ into this world to come to die on the cross of Calvary for me. I believe in my heart that Jesus Christ paid for my sins, past, present and future. I believe Jesus Christ was buried and on the third day He rose from the dead. I believe that Jesus Christ will come back again. I confess with my mouth and I accept Him now to be my Lord.*

*Master, Saviour, Brother, and Friend. I ask in Your mercy for the infilling of theHoly Spirit so that with His help, I can live a victorious life becoming all that You have ordained me to be in Jesus' name I pray with thanksgiving. Amen.*

*If after reading this book you said the above prayer and became born-again, 'Congratulations! You are Born Again' is a booklet for those who have done so through reading this book. It is a free booklet that we would like you to have. In it, the frequently asked questions are answered and this will get you on the way to growing in your newfound faith in God. You can download this free booklet from our website: www.protokospublishers.com*

*You may also contact any of the organisations listed at the end of the book.*

*I look forward to hearing from you soon.*
*O. Ola–Ojo*

## OTHER BOOKS BY THE AUTHOR:

### Provocation, Prayer and Praise
(December 2004 & 2009)

Complimentary to The Christian and Infertility this book focuses on the story of an infertile woman in the Bible, her provocations, prayer and praise. Whatever makes you incomplete, unfulfilled, less than whom God made you to be, whatever issue of life that the enemy uses to provoke you calls for prayer.

*Key features include:*
- Some known medical reasons for infertility in the women.
- Why Hannah went to the house of God in spite of her barrenness.
- Is it true that the husband is much more than 10 sons to the infertile woman?
- When, where and how to address the source/cause of your provocation.
- God is able to meet that humanly impossible need of yours.
- God's part and your part in that promise.
- Time to celebrate and praise God.

Book Details:
Paperback: 128 pages
Language English
ISBN-13: 978-0-9557898-3-0

Review:
An excellent easy to read and understand book. The principles shared in this book though primarily are for those trying for a baby could as well be applied to any area of hurt and un-fulfillment.

Reviewer: A Reader from London, 7 Jan 2006 on Amazon.co.uk

 :www.protokospublishers.com

*To the Groom with Love*

## The Christian and Infertility
(December 2004 & 2009)

The Christian and Infertility addresses one of the often neglected needs of Christian couples. It gives an insight into infertility from the biblical and medical perspectives. It is written not only for potential fruitful couples but for pastors, family and friends of these couples. It is written that the Body of Christ might be fully equipped to know and support couples who are facing the challenge of infertility at present

Key features include:
- Childlessness in the Bible and lessons to learn;
- Some known spiritual causes of infertility;
- The man and low sperm count;
- Some possible physical, medical and environmental causes of infertility;
- Some of the available treatment options in the UK;
- Choice of fertility treatment;
- Should a Christian professional be involved in fertility treatment?

Book Details:
Paperback: 146 pages
Language English
ISBN-13: 978-0-9557898-2-3

Review:
The book is a great eye-opener for all. It sheds light on infertility from the medical and spiritual angle. This gives the reader a balance because I believe every human being is made up of both physical and spiritual part. To get a balance in life, the two parts must be well fed. One must not concentrate on the spiritual and neglect the physical part. The book also reminds us that God has a way of sorting us out. The book is quite inspiring. I will recommend this book to everybody trusting God for any form of blessing from God to go get one and apply it to his or her situation. It will definitely bless you and yours'.

Reviewer: A reader from Glen Burnie, USA, 29 Oct 2007 on Amazon.co.uk
Reviewer : Ann Harper MD FRCPI FRCOG.
Consultant Obstetrician and Gynaecologist
Royal Jubilee Maternity Service, Belfast., UK

 :www.protokospublishers.com

*To the Groom with Love*

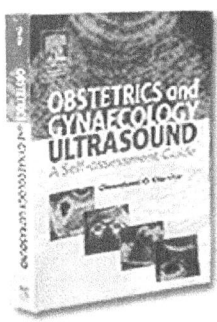

## Obstetrics and Gynaecology Ultrasound - A Self-Assessment Guide

June 2005 Churchill Elsevier Publishers, UK.

This self-assessment guide is a structured questions and answer book that develops the reader's understanding capability using a simple method in treating related topics. Clinical indications are presented with their corresponding ultrasound findings using appropriate illustrations. A case study approach is followed; presenting the clinical and ethical dilemmas that might arise while encouraging students to think. The aim is to reinforce theoretical knowledge within a clinical environment.

### Key features:
- Over 600 high-resolution ultrasound images
- Cover a wide spectrum of ultrasound curriculum.
- Includes a detailed study of fertility.
- Aids quick understanding of subject matter.
- 468 pages.

ISBN-10: 0443064628
ISBN-13: 978-0443064623
Book Dimensions: 24 x 16.8 x 2.6 cm

*"...This excellent new book is a study guide... This is an attractive paperback that should be essential reading for trainee obstetric and gynaecological sonographers, whether they are radiographers or radiology or obstetric trainees. It will be of particular value to those preparing for the RCOG/RCR Diploma in Advanced Obstetric Ultrasound and to specialist registrars in obstetrics and gynaecology undertaking special skills modules in fetal medicine, gynaecological ultrasound and infertility..."*

The Obstetrician & Gynaecologist, www.rcog.org.uk/togonline
Book reviews 2006

### Reviewer **Ann Harper MD FRCPI FRCOG.**
Consultant Obstetrician and Gynaecologist
Royal Jubilee Maternity Service, Belfast., UK

 :www.protokospublishers.com

## GOOD MUMS, BAD MUMS
(June 2005 & 2009)

This is in two parts, the main chapter that can be used for personal or group study, and an accompanying exercise section. The privileged position of a mother is in her being a co-creator with God and bringing forth life (lives). This book compliments one of God's previous revelations to me as contained in the book titled Good Dads, Bad Dads'. While the father could be likened to the pilot of the family plane, the mother can be likened to the force behind the plane – positive or negative. Good mothers are not only co-creators with God, they also do nurture as well as nourish their children physically, emotionally and spiritually.

### *Keys Features*:
- Were all the mothers in the Bible god mothers?
- Lessons from the strengths and weakness of seven mothers.
- Be encouraged - you are not alone in the assignment of motherhood.
- Be motivated in the areas of your strengths.
- Learn ways of supporting your husband and children.

### Book Details:
Paperback: 162 pages
Language English
ISBN-13: 978-0-9557898-1-6
Book Dimensions: 21.4 x 14 x 1.4 cm

I appreciate the author's method of writing. It is always exciting holding her book to read. Personally, 'Good Mums, Bad Mums' has been a blessing to me in no small measure. The book is rich, it is loaded with physical and spiritual uplifting subjects. To all existing and potential mothers, this book is a MUST read. At the end of every chapter there is an exercise to do that will help in re-examining your life spiritually and in other ways. I encourage all women to get and use this book as a guide in raising their children. You will be glad you did.

### Pastor Mrs T Adegoke
Freedom Arena
London, UK

:www.protokospublishers.com

## To the Bride with Love
(2007 & 2009)

Every wise woman preparing to get married knows she will need sound advice, practical tips and solid, heartfelt prayers, of those who have travelled on the road she is about to journey on. In this book, 10 women of different age groups, from different backgrounds and cultures who wedded under various circumstances, individually share their experience with the bride in an intimate, very candid and unforgettable way

**Keys Features:**
- Learn from 10 married women.
- Find your divine purpose in marriage.
- Learn what and how to feed your family.
- Be blessed by prayers from your guests.
- Receive remarkable gifts for your marriage.

Book details:
Paperback: 108 pages
Language: English
ISBN-13: 978-0-9557898-4-7

To the Bride with Love is the perfect bride's evergreen companion. The content is suitable, relevant and applicable even decades after the wedding day.

To the Bride with Love is an ideal wedding gift on its own. It can also accompany any other gift (big or small) that you have for the bride but take this hint… the bride will keep thanking you for the book years and years after.

Reviews:
'One of the best', This book has really helped my marriage from the onset as I got it as a wedding gift, God bless the giver. It's a must read for relationship improvement and God's guidance. I recommend it for people to get it for themselves, moreover as a great blessing for someone else in love. "To the Bride with Love"
Reviewer: Sade Olaoye "clare4good" (United Kingdom) 19 Jul 2008 on Amazon.com

*To the Groom with Love*

**Another Review:**

The writing style of Oluwakemi is unique, peculiar and distinct to herself. I recommend To the Bride with Love to wives, wives to be, mothers, mentors, youth leaders and workers. Why? The clarity, the focus and the intent of this book is so empowering, encouraging and enlightening that it will definitely mold or re mold a life to achieve its purpose. The truth is, there are very few books that have depth as well as help you to achieve your goals and arrive at your destination. Many books tend to excite you but have no depth; you read and you forget; they do not really change you but this book, To the Bride with Love will definitely leave a word in your spirit and move you to your next level!

I believe that this is also a book that pastors will find useful as a manual for marriage counseling, because many books on marriage focus mostly on what you as an individual can gain, your own personal satisfaction while little is said about the sacrifices involved and their importance. As my pastor usually says, it is important to learn from those who have gone ahead, understand why some were successful and others weren't, so that we won't fall where they fell, rather, we would gain more speed, achieve our goals and thereby glorify Christ.

So, I invite you not only to get a copy of this life-changing manual for yourself, but also to put it into as many hands as you can afford to, for then the world will definitely benefit and your life will be a blessing to many.

Reviewer: Oyinlola Odunlami CEO.
Shallom Bookshop, London UK

 :www.protokospublishers.com

## To the Groom with Love

Refuge Under His Wings

"an exhaustive analysis of the Book of Ruth in the Bible. The author combines her deep Christian conviction and excellent knowledge of the Holy Scriptures to produce a must read for every Christian, married or single. The book is interspaced with beautifully written prayers, which enables the reader to pause, pray and meditate on the revelations received... The book is also loaded with poetry like 'Thy will be done oh Lord' for those who may be facing an uncertain future or on a cross road of decisions."

Key Features:
- Famine in the land whose fault?
- Do I relocate in famine times and where to?
- Back to God, back to blessings.
- Finding refuge Under His Wings.
- A new beginning and a new song

Book details:
Paperback: 100 pages
Language: English
ISBN-10: 095578980X
ISBN-13: 978-0955789809

Review:
This book feeds the soul. Most of all I loved the poetry. It gives you time to savour the thoughts as reader. There is a good mix of poetry and prose. To look at the story of Ruth in depth gave good spiritual food. You can pause and take it in at your own pace. The meditation on Psalm 121 was good also. There's nothing like reading a Psalm slowly and meditating on its contents. The author's own reflections allow you to see the book through someone else's eyes. A good read.

Reviewer : Gaby Richards,
London, UK.

 :www.protokospublishers.co.uk

## GRACE OR WORKS?

This book makes you examine a lot of issues in your life, family relationships in particular, that you may have taken for granted or totally ignored. As conveyed right from the rhetorical question posed in the title, Grace or Works, the author stirs you towards asking yourself pertinent questions, thinking through for answers and even getting solutions for unresolved problems.

Have you heard of prodigal wives, husbands, mothers or prodigal fathers? This book identifies and defines them clearly. For anyone experiencing a crises in their relationship with such prodigal family members, this book, which is based on the parable of the "Prodigal son" in Luke 15:11-32 is a one-stop resource material to meet your counseling needs. And just in case you happen to be the prodigal who has caused your relatives much sorrow, there is hope for you in this book.

Interspersed with prayers for you by the author and specific prayers that you can say for yourself, as well as poems to comfort and inspire you, Grace or Works not only asks you questions, it helps you make and maintain the right choices.

Key Features:
- Right request but wrong timing.
- God's gifting and our free will.
- Abroad but for the wrong reasons.
- Time to return home
- A father's unmerited favour.
- 'Shut out' of celebrations because of anger.
- You did not have because you did not ask.

Book details:
Paperback: 122 pages
Language: English
ISBN-13: 978-0-9557898-5-4

 :www.protokospublishers.com

*To the Groom with Love*

## THERE IS A REWARD FOR PARENTING

Man may claim that the conception of a particular child was accidental, but in God's eyes every child is in His plan and has a purpose and mission to fulfill here on earth. As a parent, teacher, church or community leader, how are you treating the children in your care?

God does not sleep nor slumber; are you sure you are doing what He expects of you as a parent or children's Sunday school teacher? What kind of reward do you expect from Him?

There is a Reward for Parenting provides a lot of answers and food for thought, using scriptural principles to show you how to ensure a good reward from God in the unique assignment of parenting and child care.

As characteristic of Oluwakemi Ola-Ojo's previous books, there is a free gift of her poems at the end of this book also, to add value to the content of the main text – making it two books for the price of one!

Key Features:
- Every child counts.
- The making of a winner.
- You need wisdom.
- Good and bad parenting.

Book details:
Paperback: 88 pages
Language : English
ISBN 978-0-9557898-6-1

Review:
The book is lovely, inspiring, very educative both spiritually and secularly.

Reviewer : M.F.Owoeye. Lagos- Nigeria

 :www.protokospublishers.com

## Let's Reason Together ...Youths' A-Z (Book 1)

According to the United Nations demographic statistics, the global youth population, ranging in age from 15 to 24 years, today stands at more than 1.5 billion, representing about 22 percent or a fifth of the world's 6.8 billion people inhabiting the earth. In developing nations where a greater number of this group resides, the youth population sometimes gets as high as 60% or more of the total population of such nations!

Since it is also globally accepted that the youth of any nation forms the strength of that nation, economically, militarily and/or otherwise, it is imperative that this group of people cannot be overlooked.

It is against this backdrop that the book, LET'S REASON TOGETHER – YOUTH'S A-Z is a timely one that is set to address the various issues that affect young people as well as their vision and aspirations. Since the primary goal of young people is to live full lives in their societies, this book examines specific elements that would help them in this process. It covers a wide range of issues from the sublime such as attitude, choices, education, health and xenophobia to the seemingly mundane such as dreams, integrity and vacation.

**Key Features:**
- A relevant word per alphabet.
- A time to reflect on the key word.
- An easy phrase per alphabet to remember.
- 3 prayer points per alphabet to help you pray.

**Book details:**
- Paperback: 316 pages
- ISBN 978-0-9557898-7-8

Review:
This is the most wonderful piece of youth work I have ever seen, capturing diverse situations and circumstances peculiar to youths. The work is thorough, educative and spiritually exhilarating. It is a must have for every youth worker to use, either in group discussions, seminars or straightforward teaching. This piece of work will yet raise the gospel abroad.

Reviewer: Dr M Akindele, Consultant Paediatrician, London, UK

 :www.protokospublishers.com

*To the Groom with Love*

## Let's Reason Together ...Youths' A-Z (Book 2)

According to the United Nations demographic statistics, the global youth population, ranging in age from 15 to 24 years, today stands at more than 1.5 billion, representing about 22 percent or a fifth of the world's 6.8 billion people inhabiting the earth. In developing nations where a greater number of this group resides, the youth population sometimes gets as high as 60% or more of the total population of such nations!

Since it is also globally accepted that the youth of any nation forms the strength of that nation, economically, militarily and/or otherwise, it is imperative that this group of people cannot be overlooked.

It is against this backdrop that the book, LET'S REASON TOGETHER – YOUTH'S A-Z is a timely one that is set to address the various issues that affect young people as well as their vision and aspirations. Since the primary goal of young people is to live full lives in their societies, this book examines specific elements that would help them in this process. It covers a wide range of issues from the sublime such as anger, drugs, examination, homosexuality, jealousy and rejection to the seemingly mundane such as growth, ignorance and youth etc.

Key Features:
- A relevant word per alphabet.
- A time to reflect on the key word.
- An easy phrase per alphabet to remember.
- 3 prayer points per alphabet to help you pray.

Book details:
Paperback: 322 pages
Language: English
ISBN : 978-0-9557898-9-2

Review:
This is a must read for the youths and anyone that deals with teenagers. All Sunday school staff will benefit from this book.
Reviewer: Deaconess B. Josiah. London, UK

 :www.protokospublishers.com

## GOOD DADS, BAD DADS

This is a timeless book for men of all generations. It is very pragmatic, informative and honest in its outlook and aims to be some resource of great support and guidance to fathers specifically and men in general.

It tackles such issues as showing favouritism, unconditional love, keeping pledges, providing for the family, building an altar of worship, obedience to God's voice and the importance of leadership in the home among others.

It is a very good indicator for men who want to ensure that peace, love and orderliness reign supreme in their homes and all other endeavours of life they are involved in. It is by no means exhaustive in its nature but acts as a pointer to the ageless truths found in the Bible. It challenges men to be all that they can be for the good of the society they live in and most of all the best fathers any children may ever desire to have. It is based on some Biblical characters, all of whom are very different one from the other with their flaws and areas of excellence in order that the good father today might eschew their short-comings and pursue those aspects of these biblical characters that are worthy.

To ensure that fathers continually transform their lives, there is an accompanying workbook to stimulate them and to keep the nuggets found in this book close to their hearts which in turn reflects in the way they live their lives.

Key Features:
- Written especially for today's father in mind.
- Be blessed as you read about 12 other fathers.
- Learn what makes a father good or bad.
- Explore the pains and gains of fatherhood.
- Learn from the secrets of successful fathers.
- Learn from the failures of unsuccessful fathers.
- Learn what your child/ren and wife want from you.

**Book details:**
Paperback: 230 pages
Language English
ISBN 978-1-908015-00-6

 www.protokospublishers.com

*To the Groom with Love*

**Review:**

*"Just a note to say that the book 'Good Dads Bad Dads' is a powerful and thought-provoking book".*

Reviewer: **Prof A. I. Sodeye** - United Kingdom

**Review**
Primarily, I find the book pleasurable to read and understand. To the spiritually inclined, the book is prophetic and as you read along you get the impression that it is not just discussing a topic, but expressing and bringing to light, real life situations. The book is quite engaging and provides an avenue for readers to reflect and take stock as they read along.

As a pastor, I realise that most of the fatherhood problems were highlighted maturely but factually. The author provides the opportunity to receive fresh insights from what is practicable and on-going in human affairs - duties and responsibilities of fathers. Additionally, the book is appropriate in that, absentee-fathers who are privileged to read or hear from someone who has read the book, would have an opportunity to repent and reduce the number of such men to a negligible few.

Furthermore the book is filled with wisdom and encouragement for anyone doing well as a father and, for those who are not really there yet, the author offers hope, contact details and prayers of repentance. I salute the writer for effective communication on a sensitive topic such as this. The book, 'Good dads, Bad Dads' is not judgemental or sentimental, but it is timely, culturally relevant and once read, you will like to read it again. I recommend this book to all serious dads and to those hoping to be one!

Reviwer: **Pastor Isaac Ajibolorunrin**
Christ The Lord Tabernacle, London UK.

www.protokospublishers.com

## GOOD DADS, BAD DADS (Work Book)

This is a timeless book for men of all generations. It is very pragmatic, informative and honest in its outlook and aims to be some resource of great support and guidance to fathers specifically and men in general.

It tackles such issues as showing favouritism, unconditional love, keeping pledges, providing for the family, building an altar of worship, obedience to God's voice and the importance of leadership in the home among others.

It is a very good indication for men who want to ensure that peace, love and orderliness reign supreme in their homes and all other endeavours of life they are involved in. It is not at all exhaustive in its nature but acts as a pointer to the ageless truths found in the Bible. It challenges men to be all that they can be for the good of the society they live in and most of all the best fathers any child(ren) may ever desire to have.

To ensure that fathers continually transform lives, this is the accompanying workbook to stimulate them and to keep the nuggets found close to their hearts which in turn reflects in the way they live their lives.

**Key Features:**
Essentially for the present day father. This workbook allows you:
- To be encouraged and motivated as a father.
- To use it as an individual or in a men's group.
- Time to reflect on the lives of the 12 fathers you have read.
- Opportunity to identify your own strengths and weakness.
- To have relevant prayer points to help you pray in your role.

**Book details:**
Paperback : 152 pages
Language : English
ISBN : 978-1-908015-01-3

 www.protokospublishers.com

## ABC of PEOPLE and THINGS in the BIBLE

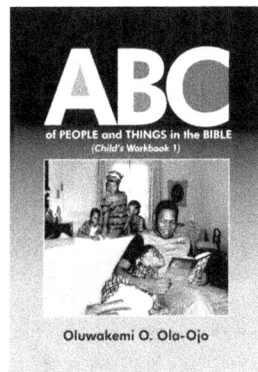

This Workbook 'ABC of People and Things in the Bible' is specifically written for the 6-8 year old as a corresponding tool to help the child learn and practice the lessons taught from the book, ABC of People and Things in the Bible. It provides a series of basic do-it-yourself activities such as reading, writing and drawing.

The workbook is a perfect teaching aid that enables the child to express him/herself and helps the parent/teacher to identify the depth of the child's understanding or otherwise of the lessons taught.

**Key Features:**
- Hours of learning and fun at the same time.
- Encourage child's self-confidence in reading.
- Encouraging good handwriting through practice.
- Unique and personalized workbook for your child.
- Easy way to monitor's child's developments and creativity
- Opportunity for your child's creativity to be developed/enhanced.

**Book details:**
Paperback: 64 pages
Language English
ISBN 978-1-908015-05-1

Review:
I love the entire concept - creatively teaching the Bible through Bible stories and creatively teaching how to write in a fun and in an Interactive way.

Reviewer: **O. Ukaejiofo.** UK.

 www.protokospublishers.com

*To the Groom with Love*

## ABC of PEOPLE and THINGS in the BIBLE
(Parent/Teachers Manual 1)

Creative! That is the only word to describe Oluwakemi Ola-Ojo's new book, ABC of People and Things in the Bible. Many Christian parents desire to give their children an early start in Christian living and discipline through the knowledge of the Bible but simply do not know how. The reason for this is not farfetched. Teaching a six-year old is not exactly a dinner date, or is it?

ABC of People and Things in the Bible provides the perfect answer to this challenge. The book presents a highly efficient way of teaching 6-8 year-olds the Bible in a friendly yet educative manner. Using the letters of the English alphabet, Oluwakemi Ola-Ojo details the lives of people in the Bible, to teach children moral values that will help to shape their lives as well as helping them to identify and avoid mistakes that destroyed the lives of some of the characters mentioned.

The book comes highly recommended as a teaching aid not just in Sunday school but in regular school classes as well as private home studies.

**Key Features:**
Essentially for the present day Parent/Teacher. This manual allows you:
- To learn at the Creator's feet.
- To learn about many people in the Bible.
- To have wholesome discussions with your child
- To adapt the various teachings to the level of child.
- To teach your child line-upon line, precept –upon - precept
- Gives you many hours of learning and fun together with the child.

**Book details:**
Paperback: 112 pages
Language: English
ISBN 978-1-908015-04-4

 www.protokospublishers.com

## ABC of Place and Things in the Bible - Child's Workbook (Age 9-10)

This is a work tool that comes as a complimentary companion to the book, ABC of Places and Things in the Bible. It is an interactive manual designed to assist the child's learning, by providing him/her the opportunity to read and to commit to memory, the contents of the book. The workbook also helps to improve the child's writing and drawing skills, and gives him/her room to explore and express his/her creative ability in any or all of these areas while having fun in the process.

There is no doubt that the workbook is a practical aid to learning for 9-10 year olds. It therefore comes highly recommended.

**Key Features:**
- Hours of learning and fun at the same time.
- Encourage child's self-confidence in reading.
- Encouraging good handwriting through practice.
- Unique and personalized workbook for your child.
- Easy way to monitor's child's developments and creativity.
- Opportunity for your child's creativity to be developed/enhanced.

**Book details:**
Paperback: 64 pages
Language: English
ISBN: 978-1-908015-03-7

www.protokospublishers.com

## ABC of Places and Things in the Bible. (Parent/Teachers Manual 1)

ABC of Places and Things in the Bible (Age 9-10) is the second in a series of Kiddies books specifically designed and written by Oluwakemi Ola-Ojo for children of elementary school age. The book comes as a sequel to ABC of People and Things in the Bible (Age 6-8). It seeks to bridge the gap between parents' desire to educate their children on basic Bible teachings and the ability to pass the information to children of such tender ages in a way they would understand and retain, and in addition, in a manner that will make a positive impact on them.

Like the first in the series, the book offers a highly efficient way of teaching 9-10 year-olds the Bible in a friendly and educative manner. Using the letters of the English alphabet, Oluwakemi Ola-Ojo details key places and things in the Bible, to teach children historical and geographical landmarks of interest as well as objects of significance, not only in ancient biblical times, but also in present day 21st Century.

The book will definitely stir up the imagination of every child

**Key Features:**

Essentially for the present day Parent/Teacher. This manual allows you:
- To learn at the Creator's feet.
- To learn about places and things in the Bible.
- To have wholesome discussions with your child
- To adapt the various teachings to the level of child.
- To teach your child line-upon line, precept –upon - precept
- Gives you many hours of learning and fun together with the child.

**Book details:**

Paperback: 111 pages
Language: English
ISBN: 978-1-908015-02-0

 www.protokospublishers.com

## The Enemy Within
(Destiny Destroyers)

An unusual title! The Enemy Within is yet another mind-boggling piece by Oluwakemi Ola-Ojo. In this book, she draws attention to how our success and/or advancement in life is sometimes impeded or terminated by persons with whom we share close relationships and, by circumstances of life, which are sometimes hereditary or brought upon us by our acts of commission or omission.

Oluwakemi Ola-Ojo takes the discourse from close families such as siblings, parents and spouses to extended relationships such as in-laws, colleagues and bosses in the workplace as well as neighbours and leaders in the nation. The book also explores the effect of such conditions as sickness and poverty as they impact on the human life but concludes that of all of these persons or conditions, the greatest enemy to be conquered is 'self'.

A very interesting and highly educative book that cuts across gender, age and status! It comes highly recommended.

**Book details:**
Paperback: 132 pages
Language: English
ISBN: 978-1-908015-11-2

www.protokospublishers.com

## Inspirations for the Man of Valour

**Inspirations for the Man Of Valour** is a collection of poems designed to encourage men to aspire to their God-given potentials. Taking her inspiration from the story of Gideon, Oluwakemi Ola-Ojo in her usual manner expresses how men, like Gideon, by giving vent to the divine power within, can rise from a position of timidity and obscurity to attain their destinies and indeed be arrow heads and change agents in bringing hope and deliverance to a people and, sometimes entire nations.

Taking a sharp detour from her regular writing style, Oluwakemi Ola-Ojo demonstrates personally the salient message of this book that we all can attain to anything if we are diligent enough to excite the deposits of God in us.

Although written specially for men, it is a book that cuts across gender. It is rich in content and would inspire everyone who is ready to soar!

I recommend the book unreservedly to everyone.

**Book details:**
Paperback: 148 pages
Language: English
ISBN: 978-1-908015-00-6

 www.protokospublishers.com

*To the Groom with Love*

**COMING OUT SOON**

VISIT OUR WEBSITE FOR DETAILS
*www.protokospublishers.com*

*To the Groom with Love*

# USEFUL ADDRESSES:

## Focus on the Family
Tel: 1-800 - 232 6459
Web site: www.family.org
Focus on the Family cooperates with the Holy Spirit in disseminating the Gospel of Jesus Christ to as many people as possible, and, specifically, to accomplish that objective by helping to preserve traditional values and the institution of the family.


## Protokos Publishers
London, UK
www.protokospublishers.com
(Impacting our community through sharing)
Protokos Publishers provides various resources for the family. We publish many life's enlightening, informative and motivational must read books. With each of our books, you are guaranteed a 24/7 counsellor by your side on the subject.

## United Christian Broadcasting UCB
P.O. Box 255, Stoke on Trent,
ST4 8YY, England
Among other forms of spreading the Gospel, UCB prints The Word For Today – a free daily devotional reading available for residents in the UK and Republic of Ireland

## IN USA:
www.eCounseling.com
Tel Number: 1-866-268-6735

## The Marriage Course
www.themarriagecourse.org
This site is for any couple who wants to invest in their relationship. They teach how to be happily married to the same person for a lifetime.

*To the Groom with Love*

**Dear Reader,**

*Thank you for your time and resources committed to supporting this writing ministry. Please help to tell others about how much the Lord has blessed you reading this book.*

*You will certainly be blessed by the other books written by Oluwakemi, so why not visit www.protokospublishers.com and place an order today.*

*It will equally be appreciated if you can help to write a few sentences review of the book on www.amazon.com and / or on www.protokospublishers.com.*

*Please note that all our books are easily available from our website.*

*God bless you as you do.*
*Management*
*Protokos Publishers.*

*To the Groom with Love*

## *Personal Note*

www.ingramcontent.com/pod-product-compliance
Lightning Source LLC
Chambersburg PA
CBHW070954080526
44587CB00015B/2301